Algorithmic Authenticity

AF613155

Algorithmic Authenticity: An Overview

Anthony Glyn Burton, Wendy Hui Kyong Chun and Liliana Bounegru, Melody Devries, Amy Harris, hannah holtzclaw, Ioana Jucan, Alex Juhasz, D. W. Kamish, Ganaele Langlois, Jasmine Proctor, Christine Tomlinson, Roopa Vasudevan, Esther Weltevrede

μ meson press

Bibliographical Information of the German National Library
The German National Library lists this publication in the Deutsche Nationalbibliografie (German National Bibliography); detailed bibliographic information is available online at http://dnb.d-nb.de.

Published in 2023 by meson press, Lüneburg
www.meson.press

Design concept: Torsten Köchlin, Silke Krieg
Cover image: Anthony Glyn Burton with DALL-E
Proofreading: Fiona Haynes

The print edition of this book is printed by Lightning Source, Milton Keynes, United Kingdom.

ISBN (Print): 978-3-95796-210-2
ISBN (PDF): 978-3-95796-211-9
DOI: 10.14619/2102

The digital edition of this publication can be downloaded freely at: www.meson.press.

This Publication is licensed under the CC-BY-SA 4.0 International. To view a copy of this license, visit: http://creativecommons.org/licenses/by-sa/4.0/.

Contents

Acknowledgments

Anything big that I've had a hand in writing so far has been a communal effort, but such an idea gets turned to 11 when putting together a collaborative book like this. I may be writing the acknowledgments, but the work of everybody listed as an author has been crucial in watching this project evolve through its various stages (an homage/rip-off of Raymond Williams' "Keywords"; an interactive website) to becoming this manuscript. Everybody else who has passed through the (first virtual, now physical) doors of the Digital Democracies Institute has played a part in the construction of this guide, especially Prem Sylvester, Kayla Hilstob, Gillian Russell, and Carina Albrecht. Past members of the Beyond Verification team have also helped shape this manuscript, including Javier Ruiz Soler, Alex Bliziotis, and Emillie V. de Keulenaar. There are names I'm obviously missing, but chances are if you've had to put up with the various things I have called it throughout it's life (the "field guide," the "authenticity guide," the "albatross around my neck"), then you deserve my personal thanks.

We're also indebted to the folks at the Social Sciences Research Council, especially Jason Rhody, who helpfully looked over earlier drafts of this manuscript. I, personally, owe a thanks to Canada's Social Sciences and Humanities Research Council, the Canada 150 Research Chairs program, as well as Simon Fraser University's Vice President of Research office, for the funding that's supported this work over the last three years.

The conceptual framework is from Wendy, as the book (tries to) make clear--the project would not exist if it weren't for her theorizing the concept in 2021's "Discriminating Data," and her work in building the infrastructure for these ideas to flow among all of us scholars can't be measured (not that she'd want it to be). In wearing the mask of "lead author," I hope to have done the concept some justice.

– Anthony Glyn Burton, Berlin, February 2023

Introduction

At first glance, algorithms and authenticity seem opposed. Algorithms are methodical, repetitive, artificial; authenticity is unique, unrehearsed, human. Authenticity, like autonomy, author, and authoritarian, stems from *authentes*, the Greek term for perpetrator (OED).

Authenticity and algorithms, however, often coincide. "American popular culture," as anthropologist Chandra Mukerji has pointed out, "is obsessed with authenticity and awash with artificiality." Authenticity and artificiality do not simply coexist side-by-side, they also infect each other. From step-by-step guides for "authentic leadership" (Gardner et. al. 2011) to highly formatted Reality TV programs, separating the copy from the original, the fake from the real, the scripted from the spontaneous seems difficult if not impossible.

To some, this marks the end of authenticity itself—a postmodern nightmare that undermines the very possibility of truth (Oxford Languages 2016). Perhaps nothing embodies this better than the 2016 U.S. presidential election, which was described both as normalizing fake news and as the authenticity election—with the winning candidate scoring high on both (McManus 2015). With an unrehearsed speaking style that painted himself as the enemy of the political establishment, Donald Trump's public appearances made him appear as "real" because he broke the rules (Chun 2021, 140), unlike his rival Hillary Clinton whose every move was condemned as inauthentic or rehearsed (McManus 2015). But Trump's authenticity, like his wealth, was phony: his election appearance repeated his Reality TV show-stopping antics and his wealth depended on his "pretending to be nothing but a rich man in his own personal aircraft" (Koffler 2015). As many have pointed out, what could be more fake—more strategized, planned, and repetitive—than a brand? Yet as the results of the 2016 election make clear, this easy and often nostalgic critique of authenticity is hardly effective.

This book proposes that, to understand early twenty-first century North American mediated environments, we need to delve into algorithmic authenticity: the historical, logical, and contemporary ties between authenticity and algorithms. Algorithms are not simply or originally machinic—and they are not opposed to authorship. The term "algorithm," derived from the medieval Latin *algorismus*, is a corruption of al-Khwārizmī, part of the Arabic name (indicating birthplace) of Islamic mathematician Muhammad ibn Mūsā al-Khwārizmī, who introduced algebra and the Arabic–Hindu system of numbering to western Europe (Daffā 1978). Authenticity, at its simplest, evokes the dramatic command "to thine own self be true" (Trilling 1972, 3). Authenticity can, therefore, be described with an otherwise-familiar logic: it is algorithmic. Like the software algorithms that make up contemporary computing infrastructures, authenticity is reliable, repeatable, and rule bound. For that exact reason, however, it emerges as both surprising and—as Luciana Parisi would argue—"contagious" (2013).

When we say algorithmic, we are not referring solely to computer code. Rather, we take algorithmic as a mode that describes how things operate. Algorithms are defined procedures that produce regular outcomes from a given set of inputs; this idea covers many realms, despite computation and mathematics containing its strongest expression. With input from the right audience, social media confessionals produce likes and views. To an adequately normative political audience, Trump's transgressions produced support. Viewing authenticity as algorithmic reveals the ways that authenticity relates to contemporary political and social moments. Users, facts, and truths are defined, validated, and authenticated by the networks that they encounter and exist within. Under algorithmic authenticity, the question of what something *is* becomes whether (and where) it belongs.

The idea of authenticity, then, is chock full of paradoxes that resonate with (and are amplified by) the mimetic, machinic, reiterable culture of our contemporary moment. Attempting to pin it on one individual—seeking their "true" nature—is nigh impossible when this nature itself can be performed, produced, scripted, and dramatized. Algorithmic logic and authenticity are two sides of the same coin. This is the central claim of the research project contained in this book, whose goal is to develop the theoretical concept of **algorithmic authenticity,** first introduced in *Discriminating Data* (Chun 2021, 139).

Algorithmic Authenticity

As a theoretical concept, algorithmic authenticity highlights the iterable nature of authenticity. It bridges the apparent contradiction of how authenticity marks out the singular or unique, while simultaneously appearing as a self-justifying pattern across categories. A set of algorithmic processes take the subject under consideration as input and the appearance of authenticity as output. These processes relate to pattern-matching, performativity, authentication, and political subjecthood—four heuristics that make up the book's chapters. Algorithmic authenticity explains tendencies in contemporary culture that simultaneously articulate the appeal of authenticity and its seeming ability to reappear in different environments and through different subjects under algorithmic cultures. The bounded nature of algorithmic logic, alongside digital repetitions of cultural images and tropes, creates a smaller possible window within which authenticity can be articulated. The overwhelming demands on our attention exerted by digital media environments provides incentive to search for authenticity amongst a reliable and bounded set of possibilities. Thus, the terms of *algorithmic authenticity* synergize each other: the appearance of authenticity shrouds the artificial and rule-bound nature of algorithmic logic, while the infrastructural necessities of digital culture provide an incentive for the performance of authenticity.

Algorithmic authenticity is both self-negating (in that this emphasis forecloses any seemingly *real* authenticity, whatever that might be) and self-perpetuating (in that the appeal of authentic behavior is always set against a background of inauthentic, repetitive, and homogeneous machine objects). This likewise opens algorithmic authenticity as a tool for those engaged in critical algorithm studies. Under many field definitions, contemporary rituals of authenticity sound almost identical to algorithms: "encoded procedures for transforming input data into a desired output" (Gillespie 2014, 1). The procedural display of authenticity (confessional social media content, direct-address video, and the like) is encoded into these performances before resulting in the "desired output" of quantified attentional metrics—likes, subscriptions, popularity, and general presence within digital networks. One of media's core powers is to make people visible—and thus the very process of "becoming" within a social world digitally mediated is that of people becoming their "true selves" within digital networks and the ways in which these networks format possibilities of expression (Bucher 2006). These politics of arrangement, architecture and design are the result of the particular emphasis on iterability and repeatability that is inherent to any algorithmic procedure, especially those that underlie the computing infrastructures of digital media.

To call authenticity algorithmic, however, does more than highlight the methodological nature of authenticity. The term "algorithmic authenticity" reveals the ways in which users are validated and authenticated by network algorithms. The imperative "be true to yourself" (or, more simply, "be true") makes our data valuable—recognizable—across the many media platforms we use. Fundamentally about recognition, algorithmic authenticity buttresses human and machinic pattern recognition. It ties together supposedly separate—or even competing—agents and platforms. It underlies personalized recommendation engines, social media, and network clustering. At the same time, it corresponds with, and to, older media forms.

These exact relational qualities make up authenticity's appeal. As Chapter Three reveals, authenticity is fundamentally coproduced: "to thine own self be true" is a matter of relation. Authenticity prescribes a certain transparency of self that makes someone's data reliable, and this sets up authenticity's algorithmic logic. It is the flipside of conformity or sincerity: if we conform by making our inner selves coincide with our outer appearance, we become authentic by making our outer selves reflect our inner torment. Contemporary media environments have operationalized the algorithmic logic of this command, shaping what was once an impossibility into the conditions of "participatory" media.

This book unravels the scale and importance of algorithmic authenticity. To do so, it explores the various forms of relations that underlie what makes something (feel) authentic, and the role they each play in shaping algorithmic authenticity. In drawing these relations together, we reach across disciplines to show how these patterns hold together different ideas of the authentic. Authenticity itself has never been the domain of a single discipline. Its close—but not identical—relationship to truth, instead, underlies much of the very splitting of knowledges into separate "disciplines."

By looking across these disciplines that variously interrogate authenticity, we separate the concept from these concerns. The book is structured according to four overlapping ways that algorithmic authenticity manifests: modes of authentication; the politics of authenticity; its relational nature; and its production, performance, and mediation. The sections, then, don't follow a chronological order, but instead deal with the different ways that authenticity is negotiated and questioned: epistemologically, politically, relationally, and performatively.

Chapter Breakdown

The book begins by tackling a common thread that runs throughout the succeeding three sections: the question of authentication. Authentication, in short, is not simply the process of identifying, recognizing, or enacting a conception of authenticity. It is also about determining the ability for something to cohere with one of these conceptions. Algorithmic authentication is both a matter of software infrastructures and cultural mores. It verifies the authenticities created through various political, performative, and relational appearances. It is not the sole domain of cryptographic infrastructures, or password entries, but instead a process of *verification* that tests appearances and performances against pre-established patterns of authenticity. Beginning with the role that machines play in authentication—whose rational and Boolean operations conveniently map on to such values of authenticity such as "true" or "false"—this section moves through the cultural implications of authentication as both algorithmically produced and verified, and how these processes play out in the realm of code, surveillance, facticity, documentation, and how we preserve the past. Authentication is crucial to understanding algorithmic authenticity because it is how machines—who, in their historical development, have relied on programmatic sets of instructions to produce their output—determine their own judgments of authenticity.

The question of machinic authentication is a subset of the question of authentication more broadly. Historically, authenticity tended to be contained within the realm of the human, something that the subject experiencing judged from another. Authentication (and its relation to protocols, programs, and other infrastructures that enable it) provides a binary test for the authentic: something is either true or false. Within algorithmic cultures, authentication involves binary judgment, raising the stakes of authenticity itself. When authentications can be made numerically or through binary mechanisms, one's authenticity (or lack thereof) takes precedence over those traits that, in the past, have come together to lead to a judgment of authenticity. Rather than a holistic judgment of accurate self-expression, authenticity becomes tied to one factor of identification. And while machinic authentication has brought this situation to its nadir, the bifurcation of judgments of authenticity has existed (algorithmically) far before computational cultures, as the remaining sections explore.

The second chapter, "The Politics of Authenticity," begins *in medias res* of the post-truth realm to outline the impact of authenticity on contemporary Western politics. The section first explores the history of authenticity as both a personal ideal and a key element of social cohesion, before moving to look at the 1960s and the role that authenticity played in its social, cultural, and political upheavals. Investigating the reaction to this shift towards authenticity—especially the criticism that it occasionally veered into small narcissisms—the chapter looks at the split between authenticity as accordance to norms and authenticity as service to the self. Within this split, there's a tension that illustrates the historical roots of authenticity's algorithmic nature. While the drive to be "authentic" grew under 1960s countercultures, being true to oneself tended to involve acting out a particular set of shared behaviors. The concept of recognition, born out of these tensions, forms the basis of contemporary understandings of authenticity and the moment of "truthy" populism that has emerged out of the new intersections between trust, authenticity, identity, and social life. Recognition is thus one of the crucial elements of authentication—it informs the very capacity to authenticate, while simultaneously attaching authenticity to the characteristic under recognition. It is a difficult concept, as the section explores, for it both offers the promise of being seen in one's own nature, while introducing the risk of being frozen into this nature.

The third chapter, "The Relations of Authenticity," explores how authenticity is always and already relational: mediated and shaped in the realm of the other, authenticity without recognition is an incomplete idea. The section begins with an overview of the philosophical frameworks that play into the conception of authenticity: autonomy, relationality, and identity. It then explores how these questions of identity manifest in contemporary hegemonic practices, detailing the work of critical race theory, Indigenous studies, Black studies, and gender studies that examine these frameworks. The mutual reinforcement of a particular "authentic" identity sets up environments wherein identity can freeze into place, leading to the algorithmic (re)iteration of colonial, heterocentric, and kyriarchal hegemony. But as the section shows, the paradox of identity and authenticity is that the same model of authentic identity behavior can also offer a map for potential liberations: when one is in control of their own identity, they are likewise in control of their own determinations of authenticity. The self-determination of authenticity provides a means to elide the freezing-in-place that emerges from recognition under algorithmic cultures. The formatted and mediated presentations of the self involved in recognition through algorithmic expression sets up the possibility for misrecognition. Relocating determinations of authenticity in the self or the group offers a way to mediate these questions. More importantly, it takes back the power of determination from the patterning, and revealing, of algorithmic recognition.

The final chapter, "Performing and Selling Authenticity," examines the practices surrounding these questions of identity and authenticity. From stage plays and the mediated image, to branding, buying, and bolstering perceptions of someone's authenticity, authenticity is paradoxically constructed and consumed according to the whims of predefined patterns and audiences. Shakespeare wrote that "all the world's a stage, and all the men and women merely players" ([1623] 2010), inscribing into words the performative nature of our realities. Along this trajectory, authenticity—grounded in its emergence in the eyes of the other—has a fundamentally performative element to it. The section moves through works in performance and theatre studies to investigate the image of unmediated performativity before moving to contemporary mediated authenticity and its manifestations in reality television, contemporary art, and digital identity. It ends by routing these works through the evolution of the brand in the 21st century and how the processes of late capitalism both play with and subsume conceptions of authenticity. These questions of performativity are intricately linked to the questions of recognition, representation, and authentication—they are how the conceptual image of authenticity is transmitted, whether that be an authenticator performing a judgment on a subject's authenticity, or a subject presenting themselves to various audiences according to a particular understanding of their self. Performativity is the mathematical operator of algorithmic authenticity, binding—and breaking—the ties between recognizers and representers, between authenticators and the authenticated. It is how the self (whether authentic or not) is communicated and expressed. Thus, it is crucial to the concept of algorithmic authenticity because it is the action or practice of tying together these images of the authentic.

Authenticating Contemporary Misinformation

The ultimate goal of this overview is to provide the background for an alternative lens through which to view contemporary misinformation. It is part of the *Beyond Verification* project, which explores the importance of authenticity to the spread of mis- and dis-information online (Digital Democracies Institute 2022).

The continued power of mis- and disinformation that has emerged in global politics under algorithmic cultures illustrates the ineffectiveness of traditional factchecking approaches. Or, in other words: fact-checking doesn't seem to change much at the polling booth (Swire et. al. 2017). Prioritizing factchecking as the only means to combat contemporary information disorders ignores extensive research into the relationship between media and evidence (the first stories of "fake news" coincided with the emergence of modern media; see Darnton 2017; also, the fundamental text, Bernays 1928). Researchers in the fields of media studies, political theory, history, and the history of science have highlighted the centrality of authenticity and rhetoric to trust and politics (Daston 1995; Orvell 1989; Rossinow 1998; Golomb 2012; Dyde 2015). Literary and African American studies scholars have emphasized the importance of fiction, or critical fabulation, to truth-telling (Hartman 2019; Johnson 2003; Nash 2020; Nyong'o 2014). Indigenous studies and anthropology researchers have revealed the costs and benefits of the politics of authenticity (J. Barker 2011; Povinelli 2002; Coulthard 2014). Performance grounds identity in ways that are neither cynical nor insincere. If factuality isn't the question, when it comes to information disorders, then what is? This book proposes that authenticity—and its algorithmic nature—are key to understanding contemporary mis- and disinformation problems.

This book thus lays the groundwork for a shift in focus from endless accusations of "fake news" to investigating why and how any piece of information, relation or interaction comes to feel "true" and "authentic". By exploring interdisciplinary histories and practices of authenticity, truth, and factuality, it offers alternative perspectives to approach and question mis- and disinformation. It then concludes by calling for interdisciplinary methods and artistic practices to study the impact of authenticity.

[1]

Authentication

At the start of the 21st century, software, computational infrastructures, and technology increasingly manage life. Nowhere is the logic of these managements clearer than in the expanding relevance of algorithms. Algorithms as a subject of academic interest rose in the 1960s alongside computer science's desire to establish itself as a discipline independent from mathematics (Bullynck 2016). They have retroactively been defined as procedures or techniques for achieving some end; historiographic research has made use of the concept to connect various tendencies in the development of mathematics and numeracy by examining the procedural texts of ancient cultures like Egypt and Babylon (ibid.). But the word's rise as a part of the vocabulary of computer science points us closer to the contemporary meaning of the term, where algorithms make up the "ontology of the world according to a computer" (Manovich 1999, 84).

Algorithms are the means by which computers *do things*. The things that computers do, however, are bound by procedural logic: it's no coincidence that programming languages interface with the hardware in the form of "instruction sets," determinate

Boolean switches of electronic circuitry. Algorithms, then, can be understood more broadly as sets of instructions with regular outcomes. Ed Finn, for example, quotes Robert Sedgewick's "pragmatist's definition" of an algorithm as simply "a method for solving a problem" (2017, 18). Totaro and Nino define it as "one of the specific forms" of mathematical function (2014, 29). Even early computer scientists such as A. A. Markov emphasized the procedural nature of an algorithm over any necessarily software-based elements. For Markov, algorithms "possess three variables: definiteness, generality, and conclusiveness ... [they have] only a set number of states that can be described and are always predictive ... [they are] general in being logic gates capable of true/false statements and not specific descriptions of the content of the signal ... and they are conclusive—either the [neural] net fires or it does not, the statement is thus absolutely true or it is false, there are no other interpretations of the situation" (Halpern 2014, 158). The abstraction of code from its material effects sets off a chain of "backgrounding," as Adrian Mackenzie tells us, because "it isolates code from particular contexts and distills it down to relations and operations" (Mackenzie 2006, 4). This backgrounding creates a paradox of computing: while on the one hand, algorithms seem to be nothing more than "encoded procedures for transforming input data into a desired output" (Gillespie 2014, 1), this procedural technics obscures the fact that "code solicits different concepts of social processuality" (Mackenzie 2006, 15).

To refer to the processes affected by code as "social" risks underselling their direct impact on political, ontological, and epistemological change. The work that this chapter covers illustrates what is meant by the epochization of our time as the age of computation, the algorithm, or the digital: how algorithms, their logics, and their technics affect change. As we become the "recipients" of algorithmic executions (Mackenzie 2006, 15), we become subject not only to the contingencies of their procedures, but enter into a tension with the epistemic bounds embedded in their drive towards completion—as well as its speculative "modes of thought," which reveal how algorithms cannot be reduced to abstractions (Parisi 2016, 144).

Thus while these social phenomena of algorithmic culture require a critical lens, algorithmic logics surface in a way that exceeds their procedural and instrumental operations. Through this lens, algorithms and their infrastructures possess a "contagious architecture" of infinite parts that explode within any finite operation (Parisi 2019), in addition to a certain "mysticism" (Mackenzie 2006, 3). From "claims about 'superhuman' accuracy and insight" (Campolo and Crawford 2020, 1) to rhetorical descriptions of big data and algorithmic operations as "both El Dorado and panacea" (McQuillan 2015), algorithmic life has taken hold because of its ability to operate in the background as the godhead of reason. The Boolean nature of algorithms—the degree to which they are right or wrong, correct or incorrect—is necessary to their understanding. And it is no coincidence that the question of "objectively" real mimics the question of the authentic. As part of the infrastructures that manage contemporary life, algorithmic truth or facticity is the "authentic" of the machine world. Algorithmic logic authenticates what it deals with. It determines if it is real, true, factual, or fake, unreal, dishonest. And it is no coincidence that this question of authentication—the technique of determining whether something is indeed real, true, factual—is at the core of contemporary questions of authenticity. One can either be judged as authentic (Trump) or not (Clinton). One can either be true (the authentic self) or false (a performative, insincere self).

Machinic Inauthenticity and Technical Authentication

The authenticity imperative dictates that one be "true to yourself," (or more simply, "be true"). This imperative has made our data valuable (recognizable) across our media landscape, all in the name of safety and comfort. User authentication was pitched as a way to make online spaces safe.[1] User authentication, however, has not made the Internet a safe space (it has, however, normalized e-commerce).[2] As philosopher Helen Nissenbaum notes, although security is central to the online translation of monetary exchange such as banking and online shopping, it can "no more achieve trust and trustworthiness, online—in their full-blown senses—than prison bars, surveillance cameras, airport X-ray conveyor belts, body frisks, and padlocks, could achieve offline. This is so because the very ends envisioned by the proponents of security and e-commerce are contrary to core meanings and mechanisms of trust" (Nissenbaum 2001, 655). This creates an internalized picture of trust, where safety exists in the hands of "sanctioned, established, powerful individuals and organizations" (662) and danger can (and *will*) come from the outside. In contrast, trust entails vulnerability. In a realm in which everything is secure, trust is not needed: "when people trust, they expose themselves to risk. Although trust may be based on something—past experience, the nature of one's relationships, and so on—it involves no guarantees" (656).

1 These arguments were not new or specific to Web 2.0. Ever since the internet emerged as a mass medium in the mid-1990s, corporations have argued that securing identity is crucial to securing trust and safety. Corporations such as Google and Facebook, whose data mining operations require user authentication, support tethering together on and offline identities. Randi Zuckerburg, marketing director of Facebook, argued in 2011 that for the sake of safety, "[a]nonymity on the Internet has to go away" (Bosker 2011). Eric Schmidt, CEO of Google, made a similar argument in 2010 stating "in a world of asynchronous threats, it is too dangerous for there not to be some way to identify you" (qtd. in ibid.).

2 Revenge porn, for example does not rely solely on anonymity, but also an initial trusted transmission. Cyberbullying has not gone away. Attacks orchestrated via Instagram or text messages by people one knows are arguably more damaging than ones by anonymous strangers. More precisely, as the Amanda Todd case and others reveal, it is the combination of the two that makes them so powerful (Chun 2016).

To untangle the relationship between technologies of security, trust and authentication, this chapter starts with definitions and practices of authentication in computer science, informatics, and computation—technical modes of authentication that reflect machinic Boolean logic rather than fuzzy and indeterminate human judgments. It then moves to the role that data, signatures, and cryptographic algorithms play in authentication, before outlining how the interplay between authentication and indexicality influence cultural narratives, truths, and contemporary practices. As this section shows, technologies of authentication are synonymously technologies of truth and of knowledge: they confirm and deny; they judge and misjudge; and they create and consume, in ways different than, but deeply imbricated with, the human faculties they are designed to augment, substitute, and negotiate. In their movement to confirm or deny, they authenticate—they dictate what is authentic and what is not.

Using machines to authenticate humans and objects seems paradoxical, especially given common sense notions of machines as essentially inauthentic or "fake producers." The general thought goes something like this: machines themselves can only reproduce inorganic things, and authenticity seems inherently organic. According to Victorian art critic John Ruskin, the machine's outputs follow from a logic that isn't recognizable or mappable to human behavior, and the process of machinic production carries over no human energy. Machines thus obscure the relationship between the laborer's output and the final product.

This anxiety about the machinic has taken on a new timbre with the rapid improvement of digital machines and their ability to mimic reality. Take, for example, the language model dubbed by its creators OpenAI as "GPT-3." The third iteration of the firm's generative pre-trained transformer (GPT) (fancy-speak for "text generator"), GPT-3 can create semantically- and grammatically-sound passages of text given any adequately robust language structure. Trained on over 50 gigabytes of plain text scraped from the internet, OpenAI's model possesses a firm grasp on grammatical syntax, vocabulary, and punctuation to a degree that the text can at times become indistinguishable from that written by the human hand. Digital humanists Katherine Elkins and Jon Chun, writing on their experience using GPT models with their students, argue that GPT provides insight into how language can work "even without an author" (2020, 13). At the same time, they point out that the program has difficulty constructing longer strings of text that maintain coherency or sense, spotlighting computer scientist Judea Pearl's argument that language generated by transformer models lacks causality and systematic reasoning (Pearl and Mackenzie 2018). Anxieties about the productive capabilities of language transformers echo questions that Ruskin raised almost two centuries prior: if the logic behind machines and humans differ radically yet they both produce the same thing, and if work is central to understanding ourselves as human, what then happens to our humanity when this work is done by the nonhuman? How can work—and, in turn, activity and performance—create human subjects and thus distinguish us from machines and slaves (Arendt 1998, 136)?

This question of mechanical production intersects with that of mechanical *re*production and of alienation (Marx 1844). Machines in Ruskin and Marx's time obscured the relationship between the laborer and the product, but they still relied on a chain of human operations. Under algorithmic technics, however, the products of transformer models are not directly instantiated by a human laborer. We already see GPT used in ways that hide its machinic status; for example, in Fall 2020, a Reddit bot used a GPT-3 frontend available online to generate posts on r/AskReddit, the platform's sub-forum for large-scale questions to other users (Heaven 2020). The Reddit user Philip Watson, who uncovered the bot, expressed concern about the recursive future portended by language models trained on internet: "once the flood gets going ... how can they avoid training on generated text, training on their own output?" (Watson 2020).

Ruskin might not have been too happy with how digital machines now also determine authenticity itself in fields such as biometrics. In these areas, judgments of authenticity are a matter of machine measurement and recognition—that is, of matching the present with the past (Boyd, Mathuria, and Stebila 2020, 30). Because technical systems cannot judge authenticity phenomenologically or holistically, they do so by comparing a thing against a pre-existing set of features. These features usually do not coincide with humanly meaningful ones, and they are chosen in advance for their ability to discriminate between classes (Chun 2021). Thus, mechanical authenticity is metrical or qualitative.

Within cryptography, for example, machinic authentication is an automated judgment of the authenticatee's *ability to* cohere with a previous performative marker or front (Joque 2018, 106). This is not a passive act by the authenticator, for it requires active intervention: while the subject to be authenticated may *possess* the required characteristics to be judged, they must still be presented (performed) to the authenticator (one must, so to speak, insert the key into the lock). Authenticating machines thus call their users to speak their language in order to interface with them. While it is *not* a shared primary language, the machine does not care; meanwhile, in cultural realms, the primacy or nativity of a language might be an element in authentication.

Data

Infrastructures of authentication run on data, yet, as historian Daniel Rosenberg tells us, "data have no relation to truth or reality whatsoever beyond the reality that data helps us to construct" (Rosenberg 2013, 37). In authentication and other systems, data are "given" and as such they function differently than related terms such as facts (things done) and evidence (things seen) (20). Etymologically speaking, the term data comes to us from philosophy, natural philosophy, mathematics, and theology. It was used to identify things that were beyond argument, such as formulae or the ground for analytically sound statements. Data are "ground truth" because they are beyond questions of truth—any questions surrounding them can only be answered prior to the system's formations. As Rosenberg puts it, "data means—and has meant for a very long time—that which is given prior to argument" (36).

Digitality complicates this idea of data. Data are no longer solely tied to rhetorical and discursive projects but also to the output or metrics of computer programs, and thus now closely linked to information. As the output of functions, data becomes analogous to fact or truth: in econometrics, data analysis, and other quantitative methodologies for uncovering facts, the outputs of calculating devices are treated as proxy truth statements. This resonates with what the sociologist and historian of science Alain Desrosières has called "proof in use" realism. This type of realism, prevalent in statistics, sees reality as "nothing more than the database to which [users] have access" (2001, 346). He contrasts it to a constructivist attitude towards numbering practices, which explicitly admits "that the definition and coding of the measured variables are 'constructed, conventional, and arrived at through negotiation'" (340). The artist and scholar Johanna Drucker distinguishes between realist and constructivist approaches by arguing that within the former, data are "capta," "taken" rather than "given" (Drucker 2011). Understanding data as capta moves us from data science to data sociology and situated data analysis (Rettberg 2020), from data literacy to data infrastructure literacy (Gray, Gerlitz, and Bounegru 2018), and from working with data *sets* to investigating data *settings* (Loukissas 2019). This shift also enables us to interrogate better the dominant practices and ideals deployed within processes of authentication and resulting automated racisms, inequalities, injustices, and oppressions (Buolamwini and Gebru 2018).

Cryptography

Cryptographic authentication relies on "signatures" to verify the integrity of messages that traverse networks. "Messages" here are understood in the information-scientific sense: not a human utterance or a block of readable text but information transmitted using any of the vast interconnected protocols, techniques, and codes that make up digital technology. The RSA protocol used in secure data transmission, created in 1978 at MIT by computer scientists Ron Rivest, Adi Shamir, and Leonard Adleman (the initials of the three's last names make up the acronym; Rivest, Shamir, and Adleman 1978) epitomizes contemporary cryptographic signatures. RSA is an asymmetric public-private key crypto system, which makes it sound more complicated than what it is: a system that uses the metaphor of a lock and a key. Public and private "keys" are created from two distinct and randomly chosen prime numbers, and the algorithm manipulates these numbers so that the first number (the public key) relates the second number (the private key) in a way that is easy to compute but difficult to reverse. The public key can be known to anyone and is used to *encrypt* the given message. In contrast, the private key must be kept secret, and one needs both keys to recover the initial distinct prime numbers.

In their 1978 paper, Rivest, Shamir and Adleman make the bold claim that the "era of 'electronic mail' may soon be upon us," and thus "we must ensure that two important properties of the current 'paper mail' system are preserved: (a) messages are private, and (b) messages can be signed" (120). While they were right about the era of electronic mail, they were not about what would be preserved from standard email. RSA forms the foundation of "Pretty Good Privacy" (PGP, the de facto standard suite of privacy tools for emails), but PGP is at best a niche tool, and emails for the most part have historically been sent unencrypted and unsigned cryptographically (Pornin 2011). This is partly because email is deeply centralized under a few major companies, which add infrastructural and incentive-based barriers to providing privacy. Further, if providers like Google's Gmail couldn't read user email, then they wouldn't be able to serve personalized advertisements.

Email is private if we base our conception of privacy from the point of the end user. It is anything but private if we expand our definition to include the prying eyes of machines and humans who work at one's provider. Password protection is designed to maintain access-based transparency, not content-based transparency, and the contrast between the two tells us quite a bit about who should be kept out and who should be allowed in. Passwords are a method of authentication: whether a sticky note pasted to your monitor, or a mnemonic memorized in your head, passwords rely on telling secrets (the performance of knowing) as a proxy for individual identity.

A consumer facing example that makes the stakes, relations, and limits of passwords and signatures clear is logging onto a third-party platform using Facebook or Google. By providing this option, a given platform or login portal frames one's identity on Google or Facebook as trustworthy and, in turn, a valid representation of the user. What used to be standard—the email address—is too brittle, too fragile in considerations of "authentic" identity, which in this instance is the coherence between an account owner to a real human being and their *singular* existence (stories of Facebook asking users to upload a scan of their driver's license to prove their identity, for example, are manifold—see Ode 2021).

Network technologies of authentication concatenate activities and accounts into one single identity, ostensibly representative of a person's fleshy material life. What might initially have been a key to accessing the Google suite of products soon becomes key to accessing Amazon shopping habits, dating app preferences, even the steps a Fitbit records (Hong 2016). The digital signature thus moves from a tool to verify identity to the very foundation of a digital identity. It echoes the pattern recognition involved in judgments of authenticity; cryptographic signatures signify authentic coherence between uttered information and its source, a pattern-matching of *n*=2. Digital signatures move digital identity to a prefigured state of being, and users must constantly prove their authenticity by cohering to it. They set out a set of rules and criteria that must be fulfilled in order to be authenticated. In other words, they judge a user's authenticity based on the user's ability to perform the steps of an authenticating algorithm.

Yet authentication is not restricted to the digital and the machinic. It is, at its core, the judgment of whether something is authentic, or whether it coheres with an expected pattern or causal schema. By *determining* authenticity, authentication is both an act of judgment and an act of recognition. It recognizes the correlation between a particular instance or appearance of something and the authenticator's framework for what constitutes that category. It matches past and present observed experience.

Human or machine authentication are both, then, questions of conformity to pre-established patterns. And while machinic authentication may seem more infallible, the algorithms and data that it is built upon depend on "industrial infrastructures, supply chains and human labor that stretch around the globe but are kept opaque" (Crawford 2021, 48). These hidden infrastructures reflect the fact that algorithms are constructed from already-captured user data. Further, the patterns against which any type of authentication occurs reflect hegemonic ideals of authenticity. However, authentication also opens possibilities for liberation: the modes of queer authentication described in upcoming chapters can also open productive spaces for dis-identification and different modes of authenticity.

Fact-checking

The understanding of data and information as "that which is given prior to argument" (Rosenberg 2013) assumes that the *stuff* of authentication is preestablished, that authentication simply works with facticity. But how does something become fact? Facticity itself has a tumultuous relationship with reporting, representation, and truth. Facticity and knowledge are often the product of long chains of argumentation, debate, and dialectical exchange—a far cry from the Boolean characteristic of true and false reified by authentication protocols. Science and technology studies scholars have argued that facts are socio-material achievements: they depend on many different things to exist. For example, facts are constructed via various apparati and robust networks of practice. Bruno Latour and Steve Woolgar, in their seminal study of the Salk Institute's work on the peptide TRF(H), claim that the practices of logical deduction that underlie common understandings of facticity are "sociologically (rather than logically) determined" (Latour and Woolgar 1979, 136). A network of material, technical, and human resources make the laboratory the authoritative location of establishing and expressing fact. Crucially, Latour more recently has emphasized the limits of this analysis—that facticity can even *be determined* in its power to organize and incentivize behavior—and instead focused on the idea of analysis and investigation not so much as *facts*, but as *matters of concern* (Latour 2004).

In her work on automated fact-checking and systems, sociologist Noortje Marres argues that these systems shape not only what is acknowledged as true; they also legitimate positivist methods for claim validation (Marres 2018). She illustrates how fact-checking systems that simply demarcate true from false risk reinforcing problematic binary oppositions between knowing experts and undiscerning publics. Correspondence based fact-checking systems also ignore the role that algorithmic infrastructures play in content selection, circulation, and opinion manipulation. These elaborate alliances and complex work are also needed to ensure that facts travel and become recognized as authentic. Sociologist Michel Callon's classic study of a group of scientists who took on the decline of the scallop population at a key fishing site in France illustrates the many mechanisms needed to make facts circulate: the problem must be defined in a way that makes the scientists essential to its resolution; it must enroll other actors and define authentic roles; and it must secure alliances across labor classes (Callon 1984). Trust between those who will soon "hold" the fact is also key. Science studies scholar Steven Shapin, in his study of the social history of truth, tells us that within Early Modern science, "gentlemanly conduct" served as the basis for trust and thus truth (Shapin 1994, 64). As studies of public engagement with science have shown, the trust and credibility that publics are willing to invest in scientific facts and institutions depend on ongoing social processes, identities, and relationships (Wynne 1992). Questions of trust, credibility, identity, and positionality underpin not only publics' encounter with problematic information in online spaces but also their encounter with fact-checked corrections, which may similarly resonate or challenge users.

This question of trust is not restricted to the small groupings of Shapin's study, especially as media and globalization increase the reach and concern of the public. In situations of global conflict, human rights concerns often overlap with those surrounding journalism. In 2017, for example, it was revealed that the photographer "Eduardo Martins"—whose byline appeared alongside coverage of the Syrian civil war in the *Wall Street Journal*, *Le Monde*, and the *BBC*—was not the Brazilian war photographer he claimed to be, but a mysterious figure who digitally altered the conflict photography of established photographers like Daniel C. Britt (BBC News 2017). While none who worked with Martins throughout his career had met him, the dangerous stakes of conflict photography make such questions—and the tenuous balance between verification and documentation—unavoidable.

In 2012, an amateur video by a Syrian citizen recorded rebel group abuses towards civilians and prisoners of war in the Idlib province—behavior that would, in international conflict, be deemed a violation of the Geneva conventions (Bair 2012). It gained the attention of human rights groups around the world (Bellinger and Padmanabhan 2011) and impacted international support for the rebel forces, with potential donors "more cautious about throwing their support behind the rebels as a direct result of what the video appears to depict" (Bair 2012). While the video's veracity was established through a series of confirmation techniques (such as comparing satellite imagery and the appearances of things in other related videos), it illustrates the catch-22 of digital media's role in the field of human rights: while amateur video provides unparalleled access to on-the-ground documentation of conflict, it also raises a host of new issues surrounding veracity that have direct impacts on human life.

Journalism

Journalists and journalism set the stage for shared social understandings of truth by authenticating events using methods that vary from the technical (recording and interviewing sources) to the epistemological (factchecking, outreach, and mediatization). Journalism's modes and mission of authentication links it to other genres, actors and institutions that similarly engage in rituals of shared information. Contemporary journalistic framings of our era as a "post truth" usually take the 2016 U.S. presidential election as a turning point in public media, a time where it was flooded with "fake news." A program to feed alternative interpretations of reality to institutional journalists, however, was devised much earlier, by U.S. public relations pioneer Edward Bernays. He proposed what he called *propaganda* for the "conscious and intelligent manipulation of the organized habits and opinions of the masses" (1928, 958). Bernays describes propaganda as the "privilege of attempting to sway public opinion" within a democratic society (959). And while his proposals for propaganda emphasize positive elements—from the conquering of the "cumulative regressive force" of inert ideas to the improvement of attitudes of white people towards Black people in the U.S. (958)—the second World War soon made clear the insidious side of propaganda's manipulative potentials. Historians credit the Nazi party's success to its "skillful exploitation of propaganda techniques" (Zeman 1973, 32). Operating on public opinion using the same media as journalism, propaganda succeeds through "the outright lie," as well as from "the half-truth to the truth out of context" (ibid.). The problems of authentication and verification are, then, not unique to the medium of news, but rather to the way that the public is exposed to, and integrates, their own role in broader social fabrics.

The dividing line between propaganda and journalism is not always clear. Edward S. Herman and Noam Chomsky's "propaganda model," for example, explains how corporate mass media—the very institutions that undergird "mainstream" journalism—often promote the interests of the state because of their profit motive (Herman and Chomsky 2002). The mass media themselves also provide "experts" who regularly echo the official view. Privately owned-media use experts to minimize the costs and the labor time needed to seek independent expertise, effectively making official views the truth (273). Journalism as a technique-system of authentication is thus shaped by its material realities.

The "mainstream" narrative of public events coalesces around particular news sources whose record of public trust reflects an attachment to certain notions of expertise, underscoring the social nature of authentication and verification—expertise is the algorithm that authenticates statements, claims, and shared knowledge. Usually, we rarely hear or acknowledge the assumptions of legitimacy and authenticity that underlie mainstream news. "Fake news" has changed this because mainstream news sources openly position themselves and their modes of authentication as standard bearers for mediating and relaying the truth to distinguish itself from "fake news" (Baym 2005, 261). We therefore arrive at the core problem of fake news: how do we authenticate the authenticators? When publics are confronted with narratives that challenge or push back against established truths—whether it is Bernays saying smoking is good for women, or Andrew Breitbart claiming that Hillary Clinton intentionally murdered U.S. soldiers in Benghazi (Gross and Green 2016), they usually cannot verify the truth themselves and so trust becomes paramount (Nygren and Widholm 2018, 42).

One response to fake news from media companies—especially those that fashion themselves as platforms for all forms of speech—is to regulate hate speech instead of actors who posture as journalists yet peddle mis- and disinformation. Platforms like Twitter, for example, strengthened their harmful content policies in response to criticism during the 2016 election for harboring mis- and disinformation and hate speech (Einwiller and Kim 2020; Donovan and boyd 2018). While this eliminates publicity for fake news sources, it does not address the trust relationship between fake news propagators and their audiences; at worst, it eliminates trust between these audiences and the platforms. Hence the exponential growth of alternative spaces, from the longstanding and unmoderated spaces of 4chan and 8kun to newer alternative platforms such as Gab and Parler (Kor-Sins 2021). The lack of oversight in these spaces continues what information studies researcher Starbird calls "echo-systems," spaces in which particular news sources are amplified and iteratively gain volume and attention (Starbird et al. 2018). Reddit, for example, recently banned several subreddits in June 2020 for violating their hate speech policy—including the notorious alt-right subreddit r/TheDonald—but this content simply migrated to 4chan, one of the many spaces that had matured in parallel to the echo chamber itself (Burton 2020).

Photography and Mechanical Reproduction

Journalism's documentation of truths, however, is not restricted to the written word. The introduction of photography as documentary form presupposed an "unmediated" representation of the event at hand, seeming to remove the journalist as middleman between event and reader. Photography traditionally portrayed the objective and/or "indexical"—it indexes reality rather than represents it. According to William Henry Fox Talbot, one of the inventors of photography, it is "the art of photogenic drawing," by which "natural objects may be able to delineate themselves without aid of the artists pencil" (Talbot 1843). At the same time, photography has been praised for its ability to evoke affect beyond the purely indexical or representative. For example, anthropologist Anthony De León argues that photography is crucial to understanding the plight of migrants crossing the US/Mexico border: "words alone could never capture the complexity, emotion, or realities of the violence, suffering, and victories that people experience during the migration process. You have to hear their voices and see their faces to appreciate them as human beings" (De León 2015, 18). So how are we to understand the power of photography to authenticate reality?

Cultural critic Roland Barthes famously describes the authenticating nature of photography as emerging from its ability to both represent directly *and* exist within a sociocultural context. The former he terms the *studium* of the photograph; the latter, the *punctum* (Barthes 1981). *Studium* represents the historical, social, or cultural meanings extracted from a photograph via semiotic analysis—it allows us to understand what the photograph is ostensibly about, and the cultural or historical situation that it is both part of and represents. The punctum, on the other hand, conveys affect directly—it pricks the user. Only a photograph contains a punctum, which creates a direct relationship between the viewer and itself. At the same time, photography is highly mediated. Historians of science Lorraine Daston and Peter Galison have detailed the 19th and early 20th century technical processes needed to generate images that could be seen as "objective" (1992). They argue routinized and uniform procedures, which present themselves as "... indifferent to the subjectivity of, for example, personal idiosyncrasies" (82), ground claims for these images as more accurate than others. Daston further argues that "[b]y its very automatism the photograph created the illusion of an unmediated image, free of human intervention" (Daston 1995, 20). In other words, automation fostered perceptions of photographic authenticity; through its mechanized creation, the image was assumed to be untouched by humans.

Art historian Alan Sekula has revealed that photography's ability to index reality depends on an overarching logic of eugenics, surveillance, and filing. In his groundbreaking "The Body and the Archive," he relays how the promise of photography to index reality and decipher all bodies was impossible due to the sheer number of photographs and their "messy contingency" (1986, 17). The photograph was thus supplemented by the logic of the "filing cabinet": a means to sort, catalogue, read and inscribe images. This rationale followed two different routes: eugenicist Sir Francis Galton's move "to embed the archive in the photograph" through his composite images and thus recognize the general type; and the French police detective Alphonse Bertillon's system to identify criminals by embedding the photograph in the archive and thus match people to their past measurements (55). Art historian John Tagg (1988) has also revealed how photography's perceived objectivity is linked to attempts to surveil, control, and institutionalize. Tagg argues that the evidentiary capability of the photograph is deeply connected to hegemonic interests in defining which types and usages of documentation and evidence are valid. Similarly, digital humanist Elspeth H. Brown examines photography at the turn of the 20th century, revealing how positioning photography as an "objective" tool allowed corporations and business interests to harness it in service of their own goals (Brown 2005). Both authors establish that many of the photographic practices that we take for granted as authentically representing the captured object were developed in response to and in service of hegemonic imperatives. These arguments point to the tensions inherent between viewing photography as a purely authentic, representational medium, and as being able to be framed, shaped and legitimized by the interests that can control it.

Media theorist Ariella Azoulay writes in her *Potential History: Unlearning Imperialism*, that the political ontology of photography far precedes the 20th century. Photography is a central part of imperial technology for it enacts a shutter, taking a moment out of context and capturing a limited portion of information. The shutter makes people and artifacts objects of observation and study (Azoulay 2019, 1) and renders them sources, trapped in the past. This logical tradition, central to museums, seeks to archive others as "the past" in order for those performing the archiving to embody progress and the future. Countering this involves refusing "the stories the shutter tells," for "such unlearning can be pursued only if the shutter's neutrality is acknowledged as an exercise of violence; in this way, unlearning imperialism becomes a commitment to reversing the shutter's work" (7). To unlearn, we must therefore treat those captured in photographs and archives as potential companions.

Trapped in the past, objects of observation—photography as indexing object—captures, encloses, and offers up for judgment its subjects. It authenticates their reality and their experience to a public for whom the determination of what is "true" means welcoming or rejecting the subject into this social life. Authentication as a technique that is called to account whenever we encounter the machinic, the digital, or the representative thus underlies the contemporary frenzy for authenticity. We are always being asked to authenticate, sometimes along the very lines of what we know *should* be true as opposed to what we know *is*. Through this lens, the following chapter takes up what, exactly, it has meant to be authentic throughout the development of modern political cultures, beginning with a genealogy through its cultural and activist upheavals of the 1960s.

[2]

The Politics of Authenticity

Algorithmic authenticity developed from an oxymoronic quest for individualism among the masses. This chapter begins from the vantage point of social and cultural movements that focused on authenticity as both a personal and collective goal, manifesting through a turn to the spiritual, cultic, and psychedelic realms. As the search for authenticity played out in culture, its sublimation by the capitalist class soon shifted the striving towards authenticity from prioritizing personal expression to a politics of recognition, where authenticity comes not from the self but from an acknowledgement of this self by the social surround. This attempt to carve out the image of the self through the reflection of others externalized the locus of cultural authenticity. Such a turn is key to the contemporary "post-truth" era, as the chapter concludes, in the turn towards contemporary "truthy" populism. By investigating the historical situations that have led to the contemporary politics of authenticity, it frames how we have arrived at the "post-truth" era, where facticity becomes a footnote to the feeling of truth.

Political and cultural upheavals marked the 1960s as the decade of individual rights in the West. From the civil rights movement in the U.S. to the May 1968 protests in Europe, bureaucratic and institutionalized repressions stood under public protest and scrutiny. But while the disenfranchised marched for their rights, a middle class—especially in the U.S.—with nothing to gain, and everything to lose, began to read this political call for freedom as the unimpeded right to be oneself. The irony, of course, being that these new expressions of the self followed similar patterns: prioritizing personal expression through cultural activity; an emphasis on secularized spirituality; and a collective turn to what the critic Tom Wolfe called the "Me" decade.

The emphasis on the individual wrought through 1960s cultural mores thus presents as an algorithmic individuality. Be oneself, just as everyone else is; follow these patterns, take these psychedelics, and you, alongside everyone else doing the same thing, will find that which makes you distinct. In the political rise of authenticity, then, authenticity is assigned by the citizenry of which one is a part: one's actions, occurring alongside others, make up the political grouping. Political scientist Marshall Berman, writing in 1972, noted how New Left movements, which promoted individual intellectual and cultural flourishing to oppose repressive economic and political structures (2009). Yet, as Berman notes, authenticity has been "a leitmotif in Western culture since early in the eighteenth century," a reaction to the radical shifts in speed, time, and proximity of modernity as "an irreversible historical force" (2009, ix). Authenticity has thus provided a lens for modernity's most influential thinkers to understand how the self and society intersect. During the 19th century, a concern with the self as a distinctly political problem emerged across the political spectrum. From John Stuart Mill's writings on the freedom of ownership (Mill 1998) to Karl Marx's analysis of the alienation of industrial labor (Marx 1981), the question of the self and its freedom took center stage. In these interpretations, authenticity captured a newfound concern with how to be oneself, from discussions of "identity" to "autonomy," "individuality" to "self-development." In Marx's version, capital obstructs the freedom to pursue a version of one's own idealized self; in Mill's, the traditions and customs of others prevent one from doing so (Berman 2009, xvii).

Berman's account traces the concerns philosophized by Marx, Mill and others back to the writings of philosopher Jean-Jacques Rousseau. Overwhelmed by the speed of modernity's shifting social world, Rousseau chased authenticity through his entire writing career before retiring to hermitdom on a Swiss island. It was only there where he claimed to discover true authenticity in the flashes of himself as one with nature. His deep influence on a variety of political movements, from Marxism to the American Revolution, stemmed from his discussions of the importance of a personal liberty that allowed for action articulated with the deepest convictions of the self. While modernity brought a life free from traditional modes of servitude, Rousseau claimed that this led to a mode of life oriented towards other people. Contemporaries such as Voltaire viewed liberal Parisian culture as positive because it expanded the possibilities for human self-expression. Rousseau contended that this growth did violence to and alienated the self, since the self became dependent on society to both reflect and legitimize all expressive actions. Berman puts it succinctly: "the good, the bad, the beautiful, the ugly, truth, virtue, [had] become only a local and circumscribed existence" (Berman 2009, 127). In Rousseau's depiction of the modern situation, society becomes a medium for concealing the self, alienating humans by prescribing a way to be that accords to the abstractions of scientific reason instead of a deeper self-emergent truth and "la communication totale et confidante [total, confiding communication]" (Rousseau 1903, 408). Industrial capitalism, for example, brought human contact under the logic of its own instrumental reason—and in the modern metropolis of Paris, Rousseau found not a collection of self-actualized people, but a vast marketplace (Berman 2009, 144).

Although the right to self-determination, happiness, and authenticity would seem central to the American project, post-World War II U.S. society—and reactions against it—fostered an entirely new set of routes towards authentic self-expression. Psychedelics, the New Left, hippies, copywriting, the civil rights movement, Scientology, Eastern religious practices, women's liberation, the bachelor as social class, Bauhaus, and many other cultural shifts are credited as creating a sense of "living as one's self"—or, living authentically—as the highest aim one can have in life (Turner 2006; Osman 2011; Preciado 2014). Key here, however, is that these routes all promise their adherents the same outcome as long as they stick to specific patterns, rulesets, *algorithms*. Gonzo journalist Tom Wolfe, for example, tells us that this was the "Me" generation, one whose empty self-identification turned quickly and viciously to fascisms (Wolfe 1976). Writer Joan Didion, on the other hand, argues that a *loss* of tradition led to an era of debauchery that was less an act of radical freedom and more an abandonment of the rules that allow society to operate as more than a collection of coincidental lives (Didion 2008). Common across both these critiques, however, is the fact that this generation gave something up—group identification, social traditions—in order to chase the idea of authenticity, and did so through a particular set of patterns and rules that spread like wildfire through imitation and cultural mores.

Wolfe describes self-development and self-help movements that spawned entire groups—from Scientology to Arica, Reich and the Primal Scream movement—that secularized the teachings of Eastern religious traditions for a newfound American modernity whose speed and personal freedoms made Rousseau's Paris look like paint drying. But just as we can find traces of Rousseau's ideas of self-determination and authenticity in the American revolution, the 1960s emphasis on authenticity likewise has a distinctly historical and socioeconomic background to it. Charlie

Chaplin's *Modern Times* (1936) articulated a man uprooted by industrialism, "packed together in cities with people he doesn't know, helpless against massive economic and political shifts … a helpless, bewildered, and dispirited slave to the machinery" (Wolfe 1976). In contrast to Rousseau's Paris, the alienation and inauthentic living of Chaplin's character came not from the rise of the ownership class, but a 30-year postwar economic boom that pumped money into most strata of the population, however unequally. According to Wolfe, this (mainly white) *homo novus* had access to an unprecedented surplus income, political freedom, and free time, creating the potential for "ordinary" people to alter the circumstances of their lives for themselves: moving to the suburbs, buying houses, and changing one's personality, "remaking, remodeling, elevating, and polishing one's very self … observing, studying, and doting upon it" (Wolfe 1976). Yet as the novel 1960s aged into the knowing 1970s, many of the movements that coalesced around idle self-discovery turned towards a sort of fascistic spirituality, where clinics and classes turned to antisocial settlements, and the psychoanalytic undercurrent shifted its aim to a mystical and spiritual beyond. The algorithm of this era's authenticity went like this: if you lived life as x, as something identifiable, you found yourself at the center of the drama of modernity. Far from critiquing this as some newfound deep narcissism of human nature, Wolfe theorized that the drive to self-actualize through newfound consumptive power evolved out of a social organization that, for decades, had mimicked the aristocratic luxuries of the past. The free time, and the income to use this free time to dwell on vanities, was once characteristic of that aristocratic class for whom this "chivalric tradition" was exclusively available (Wolfe 1976). The economic boom did not bind citizens under a singular collective authority, but instead a differentiated single authority: the "Me," splitting off from the rest of society and promising this as the way towards a singularity that goes beyond nationalistic, fascistic, or even historicist conceptions of a greater purpose.

The Computational "Self"

Overlooked by Wolfe, however, is the rise of personal computing in this same era. The emphasis on the self that persisted through the "Me" decade directly influenced the development of contemporary personal computing. The "personal" in personal computing can be traced back to the same countercultural expressions of the self from which the authenticity imperative originates. Rather than the large calculators designed for industry and government, Silicon Valley's cultural mores dictated a different vision for computing, one that would facilitate this greater self-expression in the same way as spirituality, psychedelics, and other tropes of the era.

An explosion of workers and intellectuals involved in early computing research moved to Palo Alto, California, in the 1960s to avoid military conscription. Silicon Valley, as it later came to be known, set up a contradictory situation that informed the technopolitics of the "Me" decade. The work culture was made up of people who didn't believe in the Vietnam War, yet the funding that facilitated their work tended to come from government agencies. With the emergence of businesses like Intel and Apple in what soon became Silicon Valley, this contrast in political outlook was soon reflected in the development of personal computers. The hippies in charge of the work itself viewed the potential of computers differently—as communication mediums rather than "arithmetic machines" (Markoff, 2005). Computers, as pioneers such as Doug Engelbart envisioned them, would not be tools for human use but would become extensions of human intelligence themselves (ibid.).

The technical work of computational development was itself cultural, and industrial computing soon became a metaphor for oppressive and opaque systems against which the new left rallied. Student protest movements in the 1960s were fueled by a generalized disdain for the impersonal "machines" of administrative bureaucracy. As Fred Turner tells us, "the corporate world, the university, the military, and the punch-card universe of information seemed to be mirrors of one another. Each presented the otherwise whole and authentic individual with a world in which he or she must pare away some part of his or her self in order to participate" (Turner 2006, 12). Personal computing, on the other hand, transformed the mainframe arithmetic machines of the bureaucracy "into tools with which individuals could improve their own lives" (103). Computers became, then, tools for expressing and achieving the "authentic" self in the same manner as the cultural practices of the era. Yet, as we will see later, this computing revolution soon took the same turn towards Wolfe's "differentiated single authority" in the form of Silicon Valley libertarianism.

Wolfe's diagnosis is mimicked in Joan Didion's pessimism, best documented in her influential essay on San Francisco's Haight-Ashbury neighborhood and its hippies, "Slouching Towards Bethlehem" (Didion 2008). In Haight-Ashbury's hippie movement, Didion outlines what she sees as disastrous results of 60s counterculture icon Timothy Leary's injunction to "turn on, tune in, and drop out." Rather than Leary and the hippies' understanding of "dropping out" as a means to escape the self-diminishing and inauthentic compulsions of modern society, Didion sees this "tuning in" to the self as the consequence of a culture of "children who were never taught and would never now learn the games that held society together" (ibid.). For Didion, self-recognition and authenticity might be the basis of a moral and ethical revolution, but this revolution turns in a different direction. It aims not towards a higher existence, but the loss of something larger that keeps us engaged with making up the social fabric.

Wolfe, Didion, and Rousseau agree that social pressures created distance between desired action and moral activity, and the emphasis on the individual self as the authentic arises from this distance. While Wolfe's critique sees the 1960s as a historical repetition tied to Rousseau's reading of society as a seduction, philosopher Charles Taylor reads the Rousseauvian escape "into" authenticity as a moral and ethical abnegation of the material events and histories that bring us into being in the first place (Taylor 1992). Despite this, he emphasizes the importance of some idea of authenticity in conceptions of the self. For Taylor, the authentic is that moment where the inner self and the outer world that enables it to cohere. He sees the idea of authenticity as a guiding light against another false ideal dictated by society—in his case, neoliberalism and its ideals of entrepreneurial (individual) social existence.

In doing so, Taylor calls back to another literary analysis from the 1970s. Lionel Trilling's *Sincerity and Authenticity* (Trilling 1972) sketches the importance of authenticity through modernity. Trilling sees authenticity as superseding the early modern virtue of sincerity. Sincerity demanded being true to oneself, foreclosing the possibility of falseness to others. It is a virtue tied to a particular view of early modern society as alienating man from himself, instituting a separation between inner essence and outward appearance, and thus producing the moral imperative that the latter express the former. Authenticity, on the other hand, is more than expression or coincidence of inner essence in outward appearance. Within a fully modern society that begins to recognize the constitutively social nature of the self, the bifurcation between inner and outward collapses entirely. Authenticity denotes their identity. Authenticity, like sincerity, avoids falseness; understood as an ethics, this authentic living produces a good, fair, and present member of society. For Taylor, precisely the social relations that constitute one's identity are central to authenticity as an ethics. Since we learn the language that we use to define our own identity from others, to place the other as external or separate from the construction of the self is nonsensical. Likewise, the other is necessary in self-fulfillment because some goods are only accessible in conjunction with another person. Thus, self-fulfillment (which, at this point in the tradition, we can understand as analogous to authenticity) requires unconditional relationships and a set of moral demands that go far beyond the self.

Where the self fails to develop in tandem or on its own is in what Taylor calls the "self-referentiality" of instrumental reason (Taylor 1992), to which he attributes much of modernity's apparent restrictions on self-fulfillment. Trapped in the pursuit of efficiency and optimization, the operation of institutions that once held influential and wide-ranging roles within society moves towards a central sameness, and this operation iteratively positions its subjects as acting towards the aims of the institution. This self-referentiality encompasses the alienation of laborers and the ennui of modern cultural life, whose suffocations motivate individuals to look within for self-differentiation masquerading as authenticity. The little remaining space for development of things outside the institution positions it as fulfilling the central cultural and practical roles. Likewise, the fragmentation of society into a series of institutional references reduces political participation to a narrow field of possibility and gives rise to normative tools to understand political positioning like the Overton window, the two-party system of the United States, and a generally limited political and ethical imagination. The instrumental reason of social institutions means that their subjects are predefined by the potential categories of the institution. This explains the "differentiated single authority" of the 1960s countercultural turn and its attempts to prioritize authenticity: the cultural institutions that promised mass means to discover the individual tend to shape their subjects along their very own lines. This is the algorithmic nature, then, of the authenticity imperative under political life. Patterned through participation, subjectivity in social institutions is comprised of a set of rules and procedures from which the possible outcomes are pre-defined (enlightened, institutionalized, middle-class, or spiritualized) from the outset.

This fuels what Lorey and Butler call a "society of the precarious" (2015). Under neoliberal governmentality, a precarious existence for laborers exists where productivity is no longer isolated to the realm of labor but affects the very formation of the self. Employment, as one of Taylor's social institutions, becomes the means by which the self is patterned according to a particular set of rules. This leads to, for example, what Peter Fleming calls the "cultural politics of work," where "fun" and progressive workplaces demand that workers be "authentic," or to expose their personal selves and blur the line between the public and private spheres (Fleming 2009). Through the impetus to "be oneself" at work *and outside of it*, the line between self and laborer is eliminated while the labour remains alienated—shaping one's working status as how they express some fundamental authentic self.

Recognizing the Authentic: Multiculturalism and the Politics of Recognition

Taylor's account of authenticity is closely tied to the maintenance of what in Canada in the 1970s became known as "the just society." For political philosophers of the authentic, recognition is closely intertwined with justice and, in turn, authenticity. Recognition is the act of acknowledging or respecting another being (as opposed to recognizing that something *is*, or recognizing something *as* a particular thing). Political recognition involves recognizing someone for expressing that which makes them who they are in their particularity. This definition forms the foundation of contemporary political philosophies of recognition. Like Trilling's reading of the concept of authenticity, it has its roots in Hegel, for whom "self-consciousness exists in itself and for itself, in that, and by the fact that, it exists for another self-consciousness; that is to say it is only by being acknowledged or recognized" (Hegel [1807] 1979, 229). Self-knowledge is thus not a matter simply of knowing the self or introspection, but rather requires recognizing the difference of another person in order to recognize our own authentic particularity.

Complicating the algorithmic authenticity thesis and its social patterning of the individual, philosopher Axel Honneth's politics of recognition attempt to bridge the divide between individual self-expression and the influence of the greater social fabric. For Honneth, justice is based on the recognition of individuals in their struggle for a self-realization that can only be achieved through both autonomy and authenticity. Recognition promotes self-realization by allowing us to be recognized by the other as a being that has needs, desires, and life plans. These motivations are not transparent, as the Rousseauvian ideal of authenticity might have it, but initially hidden from us before we articulate them through language (Honneth 2018). It is thus existence in the context of a language system with a pre-given set of meanings that allows us to recognize ourselves as authentic selves, and this language system is always given to us by the greater social fabrics in which we live. Autonomy, meanwhile, builds on self-recognition through allowing us to freely disclose this authentic self to others. Thus, for self-realization to occur, the society within which the self exists must foster an environment where it can be recognized by both itself and, in turn, others (Honneth et al. 2008).

Political theorist Nancy Fraser, however, critiquing Honneth's identification of recognition at the core of claims to authenticity, believes that questions of redistribution are of equal importance to questions of recognition when it comes to fostering the authentic self. Fraser contends that recognition and redistribution are incorrectly presented as binary opposites because the former promotes differentiation while redistribution works to eliminate it (Fraser and Honneth 2003). Work towards full recognition is focused on cultural injustice and the ways that people's identities are valued; work towards proper redistribution deals with economic injustice, where individuals exist in hierarchical economic relationships that dictate the very possibilities for authentic identity expression. For Fraser, then, the injustices that emerge from the failure of each to materialize are intertwined, which disrupts contemporary projects of multiculturalism and its simultaneous peer equality amongst different identities. Redistributive justice deals with "institutionalized patterns of cultural value"; recognition-based justice does not emerge from a lack of personal development, but through the denial of full participation as manifested through these patterns and their denial to some of full social standing (ibid.). Misrecognition, then, is not an impediment to ethical self-understanding, as Taylor has it, but is an institutionalized relation of subordination (Fraser 2014).

Contemporary "Truthy" Populism

What good, one might wonder, is the project of working towards a social world where all can express themselves if this social world cannot collectively imagine a shared idea of truth? If we think back to Taylor's warnings against "self-referentiality," we can begin to understand what the project of collective redistribution and recognition is up against: a contemporary political discourse where the sharing of any idea of identity is stymied by an inability to agree on the truth of what is being seen. Back in 2005, in the debut episode of his satirical *Colbert Report*, Stephen Colbert coined the term "truthiness" to describe this difficulty in U.S. political discourse. As Colbert (out of character) later defined the term in an interview, truthiness is the idea that "what I say is right, and [nothing] anyone else says could possibly be true. It's not only that I *feel* it to be true, but that *I* feel it to be true" (Rabin 2006). Colbert's character takes explicit aim at conservative commentators like Bill O'Reilly and Sean Hannity, who emerged from the A.M. talk radio tradition of the mid-1990s and prefigured much of today's punditry landscape (Rosenwald 2019). For someone to express something with "truthiness" is to engage with the receiver of said expression not through the context of a shared, verifiable (or established) epistemological ground, but to express something that is true for them. In Colbert's (satirical) words:

> I'm no fan of dictionaries or reference books. They're elitist. Constantly telling us what is or isn't true, or what did or didn't happen ... Who's Britannica to tell me the Panama Canal was finished in 1914? If I wanna say it happened in 1941, that's my right. I don't trust books. They're all fact, no heart (Colbert, qtd. in Rabin 2006).

While the satire in Colbert's "truthiness" accurately critiques conservative punditry as not particularly interested in the establishment of an all-encompassing shared reality, to chalk it up to malicious actors with a masterful grip on media manipulation is to undersell the complicated elements that representation and mediation introduce into the question of establishing shared truth under singular political projects. This is, in no small part, partly due to Donald Trump's membership alongside a class of contemporary authoritarian populists whose nationalist rhetoric and xenophobic policies stand in stark contrast to the "third-way" liberalism of the last two decades in the West's colonial superpowers. These authoritarian-lite figures (Brazil's Jair Bolsonaro, France's Marine le Pen, Hungary's Viktor Orban, and Brexit leader Nigel Farage, among others) represent political movements centered around a growing disenchantment with elites and experts, concerns about immigration, and anxiety about declining power and sovereignty, "all bundled together in the simple slogan of 'tak[ing] back control'" (Montgomery 2017).

Through these antagonisms, authoritarian populist movements are a response to a perceived sense of democratic victimization or institutional failure, constructing what political theorist Ernesto Laclau calls "an internal antagonistic frontier separating the 'people' from power" (Laclau 2014). Authoritarian populism, then, performs a kind of rhetorical homophily in that it identifies the "natural" citizens of a nation-state and claims to privilege their needs. In the contemporary case, this responds directly to the impersonal, administrative nature by which third-way liberalism mediates its attempts to balance citizenship and globalization: the mythos of a "national" people, set against the state and its power, appeals to a desire for the articulation of community or cultural belonging (for actions and behaviors to be seen authentically). This is in sharp contrast to what Jodi Dean calls a "micropolitics of the everyday," which focuses on administration and the resolution of conflict on a particularizing, case-by-case basis; such a practice, in turn, "foreclos[es] the very possibility that things might be otherwise" (Dean 2005, 57). Populist appeals thus respond to this perceived lack of the authentic in contemporary liberal state operations.

We do not need to overdetermine this appeal as exclusive to the xenophobic, sexist, racist and generally hateful rhetoric of the contemporary populist right. The formation of political solidarity against administrative liberalism is represented equally by left-wing politicians such as Bernie Sanders in the U.S., Jeremy Corbyn in the U.K., Greece's SYRIZA party, Italy's 5-Star movement, and others. The emergence of a particular "people" is thus not simply a question of reaction to the antagonistic frontier of power but involves a shared set of demands articulated against this frontier. The difference is that left-wing populism demands equality, while right-wing authoritarian populism demands privileged status, contextualized by hateful phobias of the constructed image of the non-citizen. This mythos articulates that individual actions, behaviors, and needs are visible, and that the individual is seen through more than the administrative lens of the state. Thus, contemporary populism has emerged around a demand for representation that both appears and feels authentic; one that, in the words of Laclau, makes the "emergence of the 'people' possible" (Laclau 2014, 74). These right-wing populist demands to be seen as part of a national or racial purity correlate with a view of the "authentic" citizen as grounded in skin color, culture, and historical dwelling, among other national mythologies—or in another word, ideologies.

Stuart Hall defines ideology as "those images, concepts, and premises which provide the frameworks through which we represent, interpret, understand, and 'make sense' of some aspect of social existence" (Hall 2021, 106). The ideologies of contemporary populism are at odds with an intellectual and political class who have maintained a focus on globalization and racial welcoming that is built upon economic, social, and political policies constructed along the lines of "expertise." Mainstream news media stands in ideological contrast to this new populism because it constructs its approach toward the world, truth, and "newsworthy" status through the normative claims of this expertise, and the interplay between these systems is what constructs the idea of a shared reality among a citizenry. Yet anyone with access to a personal newsfeed in the last five or so years knows that this shared reality sometimes seems like more of a pipe dream than a common goal under which all are oriented.

The problem with this erosion of a shared sense of reality is that it comes from a wide-ranging variety of sources. In their "Field Guide to Fake News," Liliana Bounegru, Jonathan Gray, Tomasso Venturini and Michele Mauri characterize the problem as such: depending on who you ask, fake news is said to represent a step-change in information warfare; an emerging form of cynical profiteering; an engine for energizing "alt-right" and other digitally mediated grassroots political mobilizations around the world; a partisan battle cry for a new liberal "ministry of truth"; an unwanted byproduct of the online platforms which organize our digital societies; or a canary call signaling a collapse of consensus around established institutions and processes of knowledge production, heralding a new "post-truth" era in politics and public life (Bounegru et al. 2018, 8). What is clear, then, is that those frameworks that build (and sometimes destroy) social cohesion amongst a group, that aid in the construction of a shared reality (and, in turn, a shared view towards what constitutes authenticity) are subject to the flows and nudges of "not just ... the form or content of the message, but also in terms of the mediating infrastructures, platforms and participatory cultures which facilitate its circulation" (ibid.). On the micro-level, political community has formed around the questioning of things as singular as the efficacy of vaccines (Hausman 2019), to a plurality of claims centering around a coterie of politicians and businessmen running an elite pedophile ring (Munn 2019). On the macro level, these communities and cultures of the "post-truth" era are all centered around the fundamental, epistemological opposition to established narratives and epistemologies of the mainstream.

But to credit this exclusively to the realm of political institutions would be to ignore the role that market capitalism plays in shifting conceptions of community, the real, and likeness that make up conceptions of authenticity. The "packaged" market that marks late capitalism (Jameson 2005) places the conceptual form of packaging itself front and center, which Jameson claims reduces difference under the form of the commodity in the name of sameness and homogeneity. This has led to a cultural assemblage made up of what Sarah Banet-Weiser calls "brand cultures" as the central locus through which shared meanings are constructed (Banet-Weiser 2012). By providing a scaffolding of symbolic structures, brands provide a way for people to feel represented and identified through the far reach of capitalist consumption practices. They provide a means by which the hierarchical distinctions of modernity that underlined its utopian vision of "securing a realm of authentic experience" (Jameson 2005) can maintain themselves in a world where even the most marginal of its subjects have value as consumers. As the ultimate form of late capitalism's "structures of feeling" (Williams 2011, 64), brands are complicated spaces in the determination of authenticity: while on the one hand they provide a means by which experiences under market society can express a fuller subjectivity than that of the simple market consumer, they are ultimately framed and enclosed by a logic of exchange that reflects the transformation of cultural labor into capitalist business practices. So, while the hyper-mediated environments of digital culture have "enabled the circulation of opinions of all stripes and from all levels of credibility" (Higgins 2019, 137), the changes that it has wrought in the realm of politics, authenticity, and truth are best understood as part of a deeper shift in epistemological ground of authenticity that began before digital culture became part of common Western life.

Where do these questions of recognition and redistribution leave us with the concept of algorithmic authenticity? For Rousseau, Wolfe, and Didion, modern society is marked by a fundamental alienation of the self from the masses; the latter two writers explain the 1960s-onward cult of the self as emergent from this alienation. It is worth noting, then, the direction of address that differs from these cultural critics and the political philosophers interested in recognition. By doing so, we can understand the impact of algorithmic authenticity and its development. Wolfe and Didion diagnosed the problems of the cult of the self through their work. Taylor, Honneth, and Fraser, on the other hand, are interested in moving *beyond* these reifications in order to retain the positive traits of self-authenticity while dereifying the hierarchies and power distributions that lead to discriminations against particular people's expressions via these means. The fact that such a call is necessary in the first place shows how we are still caught in the algorithmic production and reproduction of authenticity: the bounded outputs given by the instrumental rationality of social institutions create a set of roles for individuals to fulfill, and for authenticity to escape its algorithmic programming we must recognize each other as existing beyond them.

[3]

Authenticity and Relationality

The political movements of the 1960s and onward built out the "authentic" self as the goal of liberal individualism. But this pattern of self-fulfillment through self-guided activity contains a seeming contradiction: authenticity, and its judgment, depends in the first instance on the presence of the other. Extending from Charles Taylor's theories of the authentic—where the "true self" is both a self free to act, but within a stage or situation determined by their environment—this chapter deals with the fact that authenticity is always relational. "Being true to yourself" means identifying with and against others. Authenticity is, thus, a political concept; it has been taken up in various ways both by institutional and commodifying systems to validate or actively maintain or reproduce hegemonic systems of power. It can also be an empowering concept through subjective or collective self-making.

While the relational nature of self-authenticity seems to be a contradiction on its face, if we look closely, we can identify what, exactly, is going on with this contradiction. It is a case of what Lauren Berlant calls "cruel optimism," where the "vitalizing nature" of the injunction to individual authenticity forecloses the very possibility of achieving it (Berlant 2006, 21). Thus, the patterns of citizenship laid out by institutional instrumental rationality—the algorithms of authenticity—constrain the expression of an authentic self.

The cruel optimism of the authentic ideal fuels a reactionary nostalgia for a time in which things were simply "real." Such nostalgia overlooks the role colonialism and other forms of domination have played in "simplifying" things by "freezing" identities in place; from anthropological classifications of "authentic natives" to hegemonic understandings of Asian Americans as "forever foreign." By reifying identity, historical judgments on authenticity also concretize hierarchies of colonial, heterocentric, and kyriarchal oppressions. At the same time, as the work of Indigenous studies scholars, critical race theorists, and gender studies scholars included in this section makes clear, identifications—which are always incomplete—can also lay the grounds for resistance and community.

Autonomy and Relationality

Most simply, "being authentic" means being "true to yourself" (Taylor 1992, 29). Given this, authenticity would seem to entail self-reliance, originality and transparency—authentic individuals, who follow their inner values and convictions, are presumably impervious to social conventions and calls to conform. Authentic politicians, for example, are perceived to "say what they think rather than what others expect them to say" (Szalai 2016). Authenticity entails a sense of society unto the self. Taken to the extreme, it would seem to threaten social belonging, consensus, and reason. Recall Trilling, defining authenticity against sincerity: whereas sincere individuals follow the command "be true to yourself so you can be true to others" and thus seek to create social bonds, authentic individuals disregard others by simply following the command "be true to yourself."[1] Authenticity, Trilling stresses, stems from the ancient Greek: "*authenteo*, to have full power over; also, to commit a murder" (ibid. 133). An authentic person is a perpetrator who acts autonomously.[2]

Authenticity is thus synonymous with autonomy and freedom, particularly with what political theorist Isaiah Berlin has called "negative liberty": freedom from convention, society and other such obstacles. But at the same time, authenticity has been linked strongly to "positive liberty": the freedom to act and to control one's life (Berlin 2002). Sociologist Erich Fromm argued that authenticity grounds positive freedom (Fromm 1984). Drawing from this notion of positive freedom, philosopher Alessandro Ferrera observes that authenticity requires two things: that action and belief correspond, and that the subject possesses the potential to exert these beliefs. Because of this, Ferrera argues that authenticity grounds the "ethic of autonomy" (1993, 102).[3] Less positively, scholars like Charles Taylor and Fred Turner

1 Linked to the notion of "society" and the rise of cities, sincerity sought to make the personal and the public correspond—it sought to make urban characters as transparent as those of communal life by making one's inner self reflect to one's outer appearance. In contrast, authenticity dissolved the dilemma of sincerity (is being sincere to others really being sincere to oneself?) by transforming the call to "be true to oneself" from a means to an end. According to Trilling, the rise of authenticity coincided with the fall of sincerity during the 19th and 20th centuries. By the counter-cultural 1970s, authenticity clearly dominated over, and was used to evaluate, sincerity: a person's ability to appear sincere was judged by its authenticity.

2 From the *Oxford English Dictionary*. Authenticity first referred to objects deemed authoritative (and thus original), rather than to humans: an authentic document was a legally binding one. The move to call and perceive humans as authentic marks the emergence of humans as modern "subjects," that is, as subjects-of and -to power (Foucault 1982).

3 The ethic of autonomy dictates that individuals should follow norms that arise out of "rational reflective endorsement"; that is, self-imposed guidelines. The *self*-imposition of these guidelines is crucial because they lead to actions that reflect the individual and express some aspect of self-truth. Only then can actions *do as they say*, allowing for the coherence between action and appearance to function in encountering other people, instead of articulating another party's moral or ethical situation.

warn that authenticity as positive freedom can foster authoritarianism (Taylor 1992; Turner 2019).

Thus, authenticity as an *ethic* differs from authenticity as an ideal, in the sense that ethics prescribes a mode of necessarily being among others. Taylor contends that authenticity is not simply self-determining freedom; rather than fostering narcissism, the ethics of a "true self" grapple with and against things and persons that matter, from history to the needs of nature (Taylor 1992, 40). Philosopher Martin Heidegger, who has influentially argued that an independent "I" emerges from an authentic struggle against the "they," also describes all beings as existing within a structure of care (2013, 237). Authenticity is co-produced, through confrontations and endless exchanges.[4]

From Self to Becoming Selves

Authenticity not only requires an audience; it also implies that individuals are themselves plural. The notion of a "true self" asserts that "false selves" might exist. Dramatic understandings of authenticity underscore the enabling duplicity at the core of authenticity and the self. The sociologist Erving Goffman, for example, illustrated how face-to-face relations in the vein of theatre and performance draw out the reflexive relationships required to authenticate someone's performance of their authentic self. This self does not emerge from an atomic

4 Confrontation is essential to authenticity and the mode of identification it entails, for although authenticity seems to cut ties to others, it—to read against the grain of Trilling's interpretation—establishes a stronger relation: that of identification or possession. Trilling notes the hero is an actor: a hero is one who acts like a hero, who confronts his audience with a performance or artwork that can be "resistant, unpleasant, even hostile" (Trilling 1972, 100). The hero reeks of tragic greatness, of flaws that both enable and disable. Authenticity is a form of "self-possession" in multiple senses because it enables others to possess the self. The audience, Trilling argued, "acquires the authenticity of which the object itself is the model and the artist the personal example" (ibid.). The audience must identify the object/artist/madness as authentic. They must partake of—*authenticate*—another's resistance.

individuality, he stresses, but from the kinds of performances society arranges. Goffman, unlike Trilling, underscores the dual nature of performance, for every individual is both an actor and a character. As a performer, they are "a harried fabricator of impressions involved in the all-too-human task of staging a performance"; as a character, they are "a figure, typically a fine one, whose spirit, strength, and other sterling qualities the performance was designed to provoke" (252). As Goffman notes, "in our society the character one performs and one's self are somewhat equated" so that a successful performance of a character is usually imputed to the self who performs it. Against this, he argued that the self "is a product of the scene that comes off, and is not [the] cause of it" (Goffman 2007, 252). The self, he wrote, is a "peg on which something of collaborative manufacture will be hung for a time" (253). This collaborative manufacture underlies the emergence of the self, and includes tools for shaping the body behind the scenes, fixed props and teams of persons key to the *mise-en-scène,* and the audience.

This dramatic framing reveals that authenticity requires models and characters—at the very least to move beyond them. Similarly, subjects need to look outwards to answer the question "who am I?"[5] As elaborated in the following sections, subjects build a sense of self in relation to "model" bodies or figures like "citizen" or "boy," with or against whom they identify. As individuals, they seek to establish their uniqueness and separateness from others, but at the same time, they recognize themselves through their

5 Critical theory has long explored the formation of a sense of self as a political project, starting from Marx's concept of false consciousness and Marxist theories of ideology and class (Marx 2015). "False consciousness" refers to a lack of awareness by the working class of their place in the system of capitalist exploitation, which requires their labor to produce wealth only for the owning (bourgeois) class. In this sense, the concept of the self as an individual worker, striving towards success (as opposed to an awareness of the self as an exploited body), is a mode of being and understanding the self that is intentionally brought into existence through dominant systems of power which support or uphold the exploitative system.

similarities with others, shared practices, habits and values—all of which change and evolve with group experiences. Every unique individual references multiple others.

The notion of a true self, and its dependence on others, has perhaps been most thoroughly explored within psychoanalysis. Leading 20th century psychoanalyst Jacques Lacan famously argues that one emerges as an individual through the "mirror stage," in which the child misidentifies with his mirror image (or mother's face) (Lacan 2006). From a slightly different angle, relational psychoanalysis uses the concept of true and false selves to explain the prevalence of the other in defining and granting a sense of self from infanthood to adulthood. For analyst D. W. Winnicott, the "good enough" mother recognizes and treats the infant as a separate individual with agency before the infant has gained such capacity (Winnicott 1953). The "good enough" mother also communicates to the infant their resilience and capacity to "survive" conflict, modeling for the infant the essence of a "true" and "authentic" self, filled with liveliness and creativity. In contrast, Winnicott contends that the parent who neglects or seeks to control and mold the infant fosters an (inauthentic) "false self," and the infant grows into an individual whose facade of personality covers over feelings of a dead and empty inside.

At the same time, other fields emphasize that duplicity is not simply duplicitous. As playwright Oscar Wilde famously quipped in a dialogue between his characters: "Man is least himself when he talks in his own person. Give him a mask, and he will tell you the truth ... we are never more true to ourselves than when we are inconsistent" (2000, 203). The mask, philosopher Hannah Arendt contends, is central to public action, for it enables interfacing between different authentic needs without absolving oneself of their own (Arendt 2014). Further, as anthropologist Paige Raibmon has shown in her analysis of Makah reinventions of the whale hunt, authenticity, even at its worst—when it is used to "pin" Indigenous people to an "authentic past"—can still be reinvented anew, for authenticity lies in the performance (Raibmon 2005, 13).

Yet the performances that mediate the authentic are not always freely available. African American studies and critical race theory have emphasized the costs and power relations embedded within the "double consciousness" of being socially coded as two distinct identities. Coined by sociologist W.E.B. DuBois, double consciousness describes a "sense of always looking at one's self through the eyes of others," where the identity perceived by the self exists alongside the social coding by white hegemony as Black ([1903] 2007, 8). For some, this disparity between actor and character is painful and circumscribed.

As we bring together the concepts of race, racial oppression, gender, sexuality, and authenticity in the next sections, we will quickly find them in tension. Can there ever be an authentic self for the racialized individual who must see the world through two sets of eyes—one that validates their individuality or solidarity with other racialized folk, and another that forms in relation to the oppressive norm?[6] As this chapter shows, the call to "be real" (that is, different) or to authenticate others as "real" that emerged from the historic and cultural moments discussed previously, often supports cultural and economic domination and exploitation (Coulthard 2014). Again, the cruel optimism of the "authentic self" crops up: authenticity or "realness" are socially determined in the first instance, allowing for one to

6 Michel Foucault's concept of "technologies of the self" describes social and relational techniques humans use to constitute themselves as authentic beings in a society. They "permit individuals to effect ... a certain number of operations on their own bodies and souls, thoughts, conduct, and way of being, so as to transform themselves in order to attain a certain state of happiness, purity, wisdom, perfection, or immortality" (Foucault 1988, 18). He terms this, in short, "taking care of oneself." These technologies are the means by which "games of truth" are played with and against institutions, where the truths required for self-maintenance as a coherent and cohesive discursive entity knock up against the institutions that define epistemic knowledge.

articulate their own selfhood given adequate positive freedom; but without this positive freedom, to seek authentic expression is to widen the gulf between social coding and the self. The "authentic" racial existence under white hegemony, then, is judged based on a predetermined accordance with a set of rules and behaviors, ones that set out the very oppression of minorities as their grounds. As African American studies scholar Wahneema Lubiano argues, domination often succeeds because it sets the terms of struggle and for what counts as "authentic" opposition (1996, 66). The rest of this chapter reveals the limits to what has been called the "politics of recognition" by scholars such as Charles Taylor, Axel Honneth, and Nancy Fraser, as discussed in the "Politics of Authenticity" chapter. The authentic search of a "true self" would seem to demand a respect for difference and an acceptance of people for who they are; however, the notion of an authentic ethnic or gendered identity is neither politically neutral nor simply emancipatory, but instead a synthesis of both under algorithmic logic. As well as exploring power relations, the next sections also outline how identifications open spaces for difference. The "action or process of regarding or treating one thing as identical *with* another" implicitly acknowledges that "identical" things are not the same things, but separate (OED Online, "Identification, n."). These processes, we argue, have manifested in the algorithmic processes that mediate the expression and determination of authenticity. Identity therefore involves processes of identification and becoming that can destabilize algorithmic assumptions and reshape their outputs: the future.

Indigenous Sovereignty

The tensions of algorithmic encoding and representation run through various questions of identification. Struggles for Indigenous sovereignty encapsulate the political stakes of cultural authenticity, and they unearth questions of belonging as proxied through the development of the contemporary Western nation-state. Thatcher et. al., in their discussion of data colonialism, discuss how "individual datums ... are linked together algorithmically" to create the concept of "big data" (2016, 1). Analogously, attempts to subjugate or assimilate Indigenous populations into the governmental ideal of their colonizer states reflect a similar algorithmic connection. As anthropologist Beth Povinelli has argued in her analysis of Australian multiculturalism, "Indigenous subjects are called on to perform an authentic difference in exchange for the good feelings of the nation and the reparative legislation of the state" (Povinelli 2002, 6). At the same time, Raibmon has argued that even at its worst—when it is used to "pin" Indigenous people to an "authentic past"—authenticity can be reinvented (performed) anew (Raibmon 2005, 13). Terms such as "Indian" and "aboriginal" designate not a uniform or static identity, but a heterogeneous group of nations and peoples.[7] Institutional discourses, policy, laws, and multicultural approaches, however, seek to lock down what counts as "authentically Indigenous" through media stereotypes, blood quanta or cultural tradition requirements, and by imposing linear or patriarchal kinship structures (TallBear 2013). These are then used to perpetuate myths of the "vanishing Indian," as well as limit Indigenous sovereign claims by discrediting current forms of Indigenous life and knowledge as "inauthentic" because they do not conform to "traditional" ways. As Indigenous studies scholar Joanne Barker shows, "tradition" often disguises colonial constructions as "ageless" practices (Barker 2011).[8] Furthermore, Coulthard stresses that official moves to "recognize" Indigeneity—if not coupled with land reform—can perpetuate the domination these gestures seek to redress (Coulthard 2014). Jodi Byrd notes that the very notion of Indigenous sovereignty also carries with

7 There are over 50 nations within Canada alone. The term Indigenous was officially adopted by many nations after the UN Declaration of Indigenous Peoples to replace terms such as Aboriginal and Indian.

8 This concept itself runs counter to the actual function of oral traditions in many Indigenous nations, wherein cultural teachings are living scripts, changing and evolving in their content over time.

it colonial legacies, and she thus calls for a move "beyond sovereignty" towards liberatory relations (Byrd 2011).

Notions of "authentic Indianness" emerge dialectically from these colonial attempts to encode and capture Indigenous populations algorithmically under colonial state projects. Byrd has revealed that the figure of "the Indian" has been and continues to be central to the U.S. empire. Indigenous people are both required but unwanted: settler colonialism consistently deploys pioneering logics to transform those it will colonize into "Indians," while also proclaiming themselves to be the real and only natives.[9] For example, the early web was portrayed as a frontier, inhabited by American "console cowboys," "digital natives," and pioneers. This abjection of "colonialism, genocide and tribalism" to create "like-minded tribes," Byrd notes, constantly produces "Indians so that the United States and the banks can play cowboy" (2014). Against this reductive grouping of "the tribal," Indigenous scholars, in particular Leanne Howe, argue that tribalography possesses a liberatory potential in how it "pull[s] together all the elements of their tribe—meaning people, land, and characters, and all their manifestations and revelations—and connect[s] these in past, present, and future milieus" (Howe 1999). Tribalography thus offers a means to authenticate relationally without falling prey to the double consciousness of colonial existence.

9 Byrd investigates the founding role of "the Indian" within critical theory. Analyzing Gilles Deleuze and Jacques Derrida's work, she highlights the ways in which the "savage" serves as a generative trace within poststructuralist theory. This unacknowledged reliance on "the Indian" undermines critical theory's attempts to create non-colonialist forms of thought and reveals how left celebrations of "the commons" must grapple with their relationship to historical and conceptual forms of settler theft (Byrd 2011).

Blackness and the Stakes of "Keeping it Real"

Blackness has also been strongly associated with authenticity, in particular authentic forms of transgression and resistance. As Lubiano and others have pointed out, the notion of an "authentic blackness" threatens to "proletarianize" all African Americans, so that only certain types of bodies are validated as "real"; it also commodifies Black experiences in less than liberatory ways and buttresses racial hierarchies (see Kelley 1999; W. H. Lubiano 1998; Johnson 2003; Fanon [1967] 2008). The commodification of Black experiences and identities has come to the forefront in digital culture, from questions of the adoption of "digital Blackface" in meme cultures, to the appropriation of traditionally Black aesthetics in the context of social media's increased visibility (Howard 2022; Mulenga 2021). At the same time, African American scholars stress the importance of highlighting Black identities and practices that foster joy and pleasure, despite their potential co-option by oppressors as categorical or identity markers (Brock 2019; Rose 1994). According to African American studies scholar Martin Favor, "African American social and intellectual history is replete with examples of the struggle over the definition of black identity and its corollary of authenticity" (Favor 1999, 3). These range from the "critical discourse of blackness that places the 'folk'—southern, rural, poor—at its forefront" (4) to critiques of strict definitions of "authentic blackness." These fall, he contends, into a "pitfall of racial reasoning" (8). Drawing from performance artist Marlon Riggs and others, Favor points out that "folk" understandings of blackness can also devalue middle-class, queer, feminist, and non-rural experiences (2). Cinema studies scholar Kara Keeling makes a similar point in her assessment of the Black Panther Party, one that reverberates through contemporary questions of appropriation and the mechanical image in disrupting and co-opting authenticity. The Party's cinematic image of "blacks with guns" made visible "a present [that is] irreconcilable with that posited by the State, in which the State consistently oppressed and brutalized blacks" (2007, 75). At the same time, these images obscured the work of the Party's "serve the people" programs and "left undisturbed the hegemonic common-sense notion that struggle for liberation was a decidedly masculine enterprise" (79). On this point, Lubiano argues that the "warrior ethic" that paints Black Americans as an "outlaw group" foster ways of living that buttresses the prison economy: "black people who consciously think of themselves as part of a Black group often think of themselves as oppositional at the very same time as they are internalizing precisely the state's most effective narratives, narratives that are the medium by which the state dominates the group in ways the group does recognize" (1996, 73).

From a different angle, historian Robin D.G. Kelley shows us how Blackness' historically central place in the popular culture-industry hides, maintains, and profits from the ongoing marginalization of African Americans (Kelley 1999). Specifically, Kelley reveals how hegemonic cultural notions of the "ghetto" construct an urban blackness committed only to leisure, play, and illegal work. This commodifiable type, exemplified by the market for overpriced sneakers, is manufactured amidst the actual growing disenfranchisement of Black communities and job opportunities. Under these circumstances, the pursuit of leisure, pleasure, and authentic creative expression becomes labor (ibid., 203-205). This appropriation makes Blackness a form of cultural capital, and the "ghetto" as a space of "authentic" expression informs the "digital blackface" practices mentioned previously. Similarly, communications scholar E. Patrick Johnson describes how white or elite mainstream culture makes Black authenticity, as constructed and performed within pop culture, a form of cultural capital; at the same time, when embraced explicitly by Black folk, it becomes a sign of illegality to be policed (Johnson 2003). Given this, Johnson proposes that authenticity is only emergent as performance and appropriated performance (Johnson and Rivera-Servera 2016).

Many researchers emphasize the importance of engaging, exploring, and transforming Black identity and cultural practices from within. This serves two functions. For one, it reclaims the point of emergence from the tendency for digital image cultures to incentivize cultural appropriation. Secondly, it rewrites the scripts of authenticity, shifting its output from the image of the authentic self into a self-determining and reflexive community of authentication. Favor, in his reading of the Harlem Renaissance and its formulation of the "New Negro," argues that Harlem Renaissance writers revealed the complexity of African American art and worked "toward a critique of whiteness as an 'authentic', unproblematic, and central marker" (Favor 1999). Cultural studies scholar Tricia Rose, in her analysis of early hip hop, stresses that Black cultural practices build "cultural bridges and new identities that affirm and transform cultural traditions in new environments not only for purposes of staking societal claims, but also for pleasure and regeneration" (Rose 1996, 425). As Frantz Fanon states at the end of "Black Skin, White Masks": "the body of history does not determine a single one of my actions. I am my own foundation. And it is by going beyond the historical, instrumental hypothesis that I will initiate the cycle of my freedom" (Fanon [1967] 2008, 180).[10]

Digital studies scholar André Brock Jr. takes up this theme of joy and the protean nature of Blackness in his analysis of social media (Brock 2019). He reveals that new forms of being online, which center Blackness, draw from the long history of African

10 Kara Keeling reads Fanon as revealing imminent change within any appearance of "the black," for "in any present perception of the black there exists the possibility for an alternative organization of sociality to appear, one that would not support the black's appearance and that, therefore, would break the chains which bind the black to the past (as a slave), freeing the black man from himself by revealing that one's present perception of him (a perception of the past) is inconsistent with the black's new situation. Fanon's formulation of the temporality in which the black exists corresponds to Bergson's understanding of temporality, which Deleuze reveals as cinematic" (Keeling 2007, 70).

 American engagement with technology. Afrofuturism similarly conceptualizes and traces Black engagements with speculation and technology, often by highlighting the contributions of Black technology, developers, and community members. Afrofuturist critical analyses take on oppressive notions of authentic Blackness as disconnected from development, online culture, and technology.[11]

Importantly, like the "Indian," "authentic Blackness" resonates widely. As African American studies scholar Cynthia Young shows us through her analysis of conservative white TV host Glenn Beck's embrace of civil rights hero Martin Luther Jr., the civil rights movement has become the "*lingua franca* for most US social and political issues since the 1960s" (Young 2019, 95). The fact that Korean-Americans with guns wore Malcolm X t-shirts with "by any means necessary" during the L.A. uprising also reveals the surprising ways in which what Keeling calls the cinematic image of "Blacks with guns" has become common sense (Keeling 2007, 68), while the widespread support for #BLM by K-pop fans reveals more positive co-relations (Shreyas 2020).

Asian American Identity and the Inauthentic

Asian Americans and Canadians—regardless of their ethnicity, citizenship status and nationality—have been at best ambivalently assimilated in the U.S. and Canada (Leon 2020; Palumbo-Liu 1999; Le 2019). For example, when white figure skater Tara Lipinski beat fellow American skater Michelle Kwan during the 1998 Olympics, MSNBC's headline read "American

11 Afrofuturism seeks to reclaim the research and development of a "futures industry" (Eshun 2003) that, as currently emergent from oppressive social systems and histories, can only evolve to continue a colonialist or imperial mission. As Hope Wabuke explains, Afrofurists claim that such renderings "lack room to conceive of Blackness outside of the Black American diaspora *or* a Blackness independent from any relationship to whiteness, erasing the long history of Blackness that existed before the centuries of violent oppression by whiteness" (Wabuke 2020).

Beats Out Kwan" (Sorensen 1998). Similarly, hate crimes against "Asian looking people" soared during the COVID-19 pandemic in the U.S. and Canada, in line with a former U.S. president's accusations that the Chinese were responsible for "kung flu" (Gover, Harper, and Langton 2020).

As Asian American studies scholar David Palumbo-Liu and others have argued, the long history of exclusion laws, internments, lynchings, and property destruction have made Asian immigrants, unlike their white counterparts, "forever foreign" (Palumbo-Liu 1999). This foreignness has emerged through a variety of political projects. Through Chinese Exclusion Acts, Chinese citizens were barred entry into Canada and the U.S. from the early 1920s until after WWII—and before this, they were subject to head taxes. Japanese Americans and Japanese Canadians on the west coast of these countries were interned during World War II, regardless of their citizenship status. Asian immigrants in the U.S. were denied the ability to naturalize until the 1940s because they were not white or black (Heritage 2021). Performance studies scholar Karen Shimakawa has described this process as "national abjection." Asian Americanness, she argues, emerges through "an attempt to circumscribe and radically differentiate something that, although deemed repulsively *other* is, paradoxically, at some fundamental level, an undifferentiable part of the whole" (Shimakawa 2002, 1). Drawing from Julia Kristeva's definition of the abject as a "frontier," she further contends, "read as abject, Asian Americanness thus occupies a role both necessary to and mutually constitutive of national subject formation" (ibid., 3). That is, the definition of "authentic Americanness" depends on the abjection of Asian Americans.

Asian American studies scholar Anne A. Cheng similarly draws from psychoanalytic mechanisms of identification, in particular melancholia, to explain racialization. Most pointedly, she argues that racial melancholia is both the technology and nightmare of the American Dream (Cheng 2001). As she explains, "on the one side, white American identity and its authority is secured through the melancholic introjection of racial others that it can neither fully relinquish nor accommodate and whose ghostly presence nonetheless guarantees its centrality" (124). For example, segregationists, even as they seek to live only among people "like them," hold onto racist images of others, whom they define themselves against. On the other side, Cheng further explains, "the racial other (the so-called melancholic object) also suffers from racial melancholia whereby his or her racial identity is imaginatively reinforced through the introjection of a lost, never-possible perfection, an inarticulable loss that comes to inform the individual's sense of his or her own subjectivity" (xi). The "doll test," for example, revealed how black children growing up in the era of overt segregation identified with and valued "white dolls" over black ones; the question behind this test repeats in digital cultures through events like the racist backlash against Black actress Halle Bailey's leading role in the live-action adaptation of the *Little Mermaid* movie, whose protagonist was originally drawn white (Gulla 2022). Drawing from this work, Cheng argues that there are deep-seated, intangible, psychical consequences for people who live in a society that privileges an ideal they can never be. Importantly, this form of racial melancholia does not refer to loss of authenticity *per se*, but to an ongoing conscious negotiation with loss and imposed modes of authentic life.

Although Cheng formulated "the melancholy of race" in terms of both black and Asian American identity, Asian American studies scholar David Eng and psychoanalyst Shinnee Han use this concept to explain how the "model minority" myth shapes Asian American identity. "Asian Americans," they write, "are forced to mimic the model minority stereotype in order to be recognized by mainstream society—in order to be seen at all" (Eng and Han 2019, 45). However, to the extent that this mimicry of the model minority stereotype functions only to estrange Asian Americans from mainstream norms and ideals (as well as their own histories), mimicry and the model minority myth distance Asian Americans from the mimetic ideals of the nation. Focusing on the experiences of more recent immigrants, Eng and Han also argue that the twin acceptance of the model minority stereotype and color-blind racism causes a form of racial dissociation, which puts the true self at risk, for these subjects must continue to deny the racism around them and their own experiences to survive. Han and Eng frame this dissociation—stemming from the question "how does it feel to be a solution?"—as the flip side of W. E. B. Dubois' question: "How does it feel to be a problem?" (124-5).

Shimakawa points to Asian American theater as a key site for analysis and intervention: "the very fact that there is a body onstage, an actor who, all tacitly agree, is enacting a role/identity that is not 'her own' necessarily implies a threat (and tacit acceptance) of the destabilization of the opposition between (to paraphrase Butler) bodies that matter and bodies that don't" (2002, 19). The appearance of the multiplicity of selves, then, becomes the grounds for change.

Latino/a Studies and Mestiza

Yet authenticity's capability of othering does not always operate upon such clear cultural-racial lines. Mestiza, or mestizaje, for example, names the mixed racial and cultural identities that emerged from the Spanish Conquest. Mestizo references populations of combined European and Indigenous American descent, "a cultural identity that has become a lens for examining existing and emerging patterns of the mixing of peoples and cultures of Mexico" and Latin America (Young 2014, 26). The term highlights how identities of the global south have been historically constructed at the expense of Indigenous civilizations and upon the cultural desecration brought about by colonialism. The subsequent wealth of this exploitation and dispossession inevitably funneled to Europe and, in turn, the newly settled and developing "Americans" of the north, affecting the cultural and economic stability and autonomy of populations of the global south (Wirth 2014, 35).

After the Spanish Crown deployed the Catholic church to pacify and Christianize Indigenous peoples, the Creoles—people of Spanish descent born in the Americas who understood themselves as the natural nobility of "New Spain"—established an exploitative caste system where Indigenous peoples were infantilized and the Mestizaje "became the center of the revolutionary struggle" (Wirth 2014, 32). The Mestizaje were afforded partial monetary and educational advances over Indigenous peoples in the effort to bring about a more "civilized" nation, an attempt to modify or control the variables at hand in the algorithmic logic at the root of the Spanish nation-building project. This classing likewise served to draw a distinction between races, a blood quanta based again on hegemonic determinations of authenticity. Pushing back against US imperialism and Anglo-Saxon notions of mixed-race identity as degenerate, revolutionary intellectuals of Mexico's new nationalist project attempted to revalue racial mixture—and, in turn, reclaim control over the predictive elements of racial classification. Intellectuals like José Vasconcelos, for example, believed that it was the "multiplications of historical experience," its discontinuity and heterogeneity, that impeded Mexico's progress (Alonso 2004, 464); hence, mestizo nationalism was the "the only way to create homogeneity out of heterogeneity, unity out of fragmentation" (462).

Drawing from Vasconcelos' "one mestizo race" for the construction of a "raza cosmica," the mestizaje political identity has evolved from a colonial-era categorization to a more nuanced and complex ideology. Political scientist Rex Wirth writes that the most prevalent notion of mestizaje sees cultural differences dissolving into one universal identity under the umbrella of universal egalitarianism (Wirth 2014). Such neutral casting, however, carries a discriminatory subtext since otherness becomes "something that must disappear in favor of the nation, development, and social peace projects" (107). Mestizaje becomes, then, a political identity to uphold the "national project" by systematically producing and reproducing cultural and ethnic marginalization (108-9). The authentic, here, is thus a reclamation of self-determination through the very legal and institutional frameworks that seek to disempower through identification.

Scholars such as Gloria Anzaldúa have since attempted to reclaim and resuscitate mestizaje in the contemporary context. Mestizaje reflect identities that emerge from "borderlands" and thus involve the housing and negotiating of multiple cultural identities and worlds. For Anzaldúa, la mestiza emerges from "una herida abierto," or an open wound, "where the third world grates against the first and bleeds" (1999, 25). A by-product of the "lifeblood" from these points of contact, mestiza emerge from what Anzaldúa calls the "border culture" of a conceptual third country: "In a state of perpetual transition," she writes, "the mestiza faces the dilemma of the mixed breed: which collectivity does the daughter of a dark-skinned mother listen to?" (100). Hence, for Anzaldúa, mestiza is characterized by movement, learning how to juggle cultures, to code switch, and remain flexible in order to "stretch the psyche horizontally and vertically" (101).

The notion of a "naturally" authentic whiteness—white as human—underlies white supremacy, contemporary hegemonic practices, and colorblind racism. Historically, whiteness defines itself against an imagined blackness, or what Toni Morrison calls "American Africanism" (Morrison 1993). As James Baldwin, W.E.B Dubois and other African American writers have pointed out, the so-called "race problem" or "black problem" within the U.S. is really a white problem—the codification and underclassing of racialized bodies always reflects the desires and hegemony of whiteness (Baldwin 1965). The culturally constructed nature of whiteness and its power is best illustrated by a contemporary paradox of the politics of recognition: the identification of underclass existence under neoliberal regimes have been co-opted by emergent white supremacism on digital media. These movements distinguish themselves from older forms of white supremacism by adopting the political tactics and rhetorical social positioning of the groups they seek to disenfranchise (Burton 2022).

Default Whiteness

Researchers across disciplines have explained how whiteness masks and fosters domination. Historian Grace Elizabeth Hale underscores the importance of space and movement in her study of early 20th-century U.S. segregation and the creation of a "mass cultural" form of whiteness, where segregation sought to tie race to space—to bind black Americans to certain inferior spaces in order to "contain" the effects of black emancipation (Hale 1999). Similarly, queer theorist Sara Ahmed contends that whiteness is an "ongoing and unfinished history, which orientates bodies in specific directions" (Ahmed 2007, 150). As an "institutional habit," it enables certain bodies to feel "at home" or "comfortable" as they take up space, while placing others within an additional "racial-epidermic schema" that halts their movement (159-161). The algorithmic logic of default whiteness is worth drawing out explicitly. As a habit or history that "orientates bodies in specific directions," default whiteness takes particular cultural mores as the "defaults" that inform the algorithmic formatting of subjects under white hegemony. Within so-called color-blind systems, whiteness becomes what Bonilla-Silva calls a "white habitus," a "racialized, uninterrupted socialization process that conditions and creates whites' racial taste, perceptions, feelings, and emotions and their views on racial matters" (Bonilla-Silva [2003] 2018, 121). Sociologist Ruth Frankenburg describes this whiteness as a "standpoint," the experiential position from which white people look at the world and claim a racial innocence.[12] Colorblind

12 Interviews allow Frankenburg to map these discursive repertoires that describe her respondents' varied strategies for thinking through race. These vary based on respondents' economic positionality or proximity to whiteness and non-whiteness, e.g., whether they have non-white family (Frankenberg 1993, 188). While this theoretical framing enables Frankenburg's discourse-analysis methodology to implicate relations between discourse

racism, then, is the instrumental rationality of white hegemony. It perpetuates a form of whiteness which, while not hewing to the lines of racism as hateful behavior, does not question systems of racial hierarchy.[13]

As indicated by these studies in critical race and critical whiteness studies, whiteness is a historical concept, whose membership changes through time (Haney-López 1996). Drawing from DuBois, American Studies scholar David Roediger describes whiteness as a "public and psychological wage" that compensates for low wages and that prevents solidarity with black workers (Roediger 2007, 12). Whiteness and property share a common premise—the right to exclude (Harris 1993), and whiteness as property has historically been tied to social gains in the Western world. Whiteness as property enshrines "the status quo as a neutral baseline, while masking the maintenance of white privilege and domination" (1715). This legal supremacy of whiteness does not end at the level of analogy. The erasure of Indigenousness and a cultivated immersion into "Whiteness" has been encoded into policies like Canada's Indian Act. These laws implemented measures to

and more material landscapes of racial hierarchy—whether geographic (43-71), economic, interpersonal (102-134), or bodily (92-101)—Frankenburg notes that racializing discourses shape, but do not fully constrain, the outcome of social contexts of racial production and authentication (53). She infers that a primarily discursive focus analyzing the authenticating effects of whiteness is limited in its ability to account for the assemblage of factors that contribute to racializing conditions. Subsequently, she urges pairing studies of the discursive emergence of white subjects with ones of material factors which shape these racializing repertoires and reside in historical and contemporary political processes (190, 241).

13 Storytelling, Bonilla-Silva notes, often represents moments of ideological formation, where the subject is least aware they are using a particular framework to convey meaning to the story in racializing ways. It was common for the white people he interviewed to employ the trope that they "didn't get a job because of affirmative action" (Bonilla-Silva [2003] 2018). Stories like these by respondents make such a narrative feel real and true through constant re-tellings and other encounters with the world which they can use as "proof" of the narrative. This process induced by social settings and interactions play out in relation to histories of segregation.

 ensure that Indigenous peoples would lose connection to their national cultures and lose their status as recognized Indigenous peoples—the goal was to make "the Indian" disappear, to filter it through algorithmic whiteness according to what the Canadian government viewed as a "citizen."[14]

Gender and Feminism

Authenticity is both an analytic and site of critique for many schools of feminist thought and action. Some feminists believe in an authentically female or "essentialist" world view, and this grounds their critiques and attempts to remake or abolish patriarchal structures of violence and accumulation (MacKinnon 1987; Daly 1999). Other schools of feminist analysis and activism understand gender, sexuality, and their intersectional connections to race, class, ethnicity, ability, and identity, to be based on false and simple binaries that suppress and oppress human potential (Crenshaw 1994; Butler 2006). Feminists of the latter school believe that authenticity is not tied to essentialist notions of sex or binary opposition but is instead mobile, intersectional, and performative. This performative view of sex reflects the algorithmic nature of authentic sexual embodiment. While sex may be performed and enacted, the tendency of cultural institutions and systems to format or incentivize particular modes of expressing them aligns with the thesis of algorithmic authenticity: a mode of unique self-expression that is subject to initial constraints and action paths before it results in an output

14 Some of these measures of producing whiteness included: renaming individuals with European names; federal permission for reserves (land allocated to Indigenous people in Canada) to be expropriated for public works; encouragement of voluntary and enforced enfranchisement (loss of status rights); and revoking status from Indigenous women if they married white men, or from Indigenous men if they were absent from reserve lands for several months (Joseph 2018). In different contexts, whiteness, Blackness, Latinx identity and Indigeneity are produced and authenticated historically and contemporarily through various legal and linguistic avenues that prioritize white landownership and entitlement to colonial occupation.

(self-reflexive and externalized expression). Indeed, feminist researchers in a wide variety of disciplines initially embraced "gender" as a term to displace "sex" and thus essentialist, or biologically based, notions of femininity. To say that gender is culturally produced is not to say that all gender expressions are inauthentic or anti-normative but rather to emphasize the importance of experience or becoming to inhabiting gender. As Simone de Beauvoir quipped in *The Second Sex*, "one is not born, but rather becomes, a woman" ([1949] 2011, 330). Drawing from this, gender studies begins from the premise that gender does not equal sex. As queer theorist Gayle Rubin claims, "sex is sex, but what counts as sex is equally culturally determined and obtained. Every society also has a sex/gender system—a set of arrangements by which the biological raw material of human sex and procreation is shaped by human, social intervention and satisfied in a conventional manner, no matter how bizarre some of the conventions may be" (Rubin 2011, 32). Queer theorist Judith Butler has most influentially analyzed these conventions and habitual repetitions in her description of gender as performative (1988). Gender, she argues, is "real only to the extent that it is performed." "Natural" or "essential" identities are "manufactured through a sustained set of acts, positioned through the gendered stylization of the body ... what we take to be an 'internal' feature of ourselves is one that we anticipate and produce through certain bodily acts, at an extreme, [a] hallucinatory effect of naturalized gestures" (1988, 519). In other words, externally learned ways of being are laundered as internal knowledge of the authentic self. Patterns of gender performativity are both introspectable and performable, realizing themselves as algorithmic scripts that allow for slight internal variations that nevertheless iteratively build the criteria of "authentic" gender expression. These gestures and constant actions are erased or forgotten as they congeal into a pained yet supposedly "comfortable" fixed identity. As Sara Ahmed claims, "regulative norms function, in a way, as repetitive strain injuries" (Ahmed 2014, 145); instead of the RSI of norm boundaries, Butler provides performances such as drag and femme-butch, those normally condemned as "bad copies," as ways to redraw and intervene into dominant representations of gender (Kotz 1992).

Feminist theorists have also challenged algorithmic conceptions of authentic gender through notions of becoming. In philosophical terms, becoming refers to ongoing micro-processes that compose a given state of being or identity, like gender.[15] The gestures and practices of becoming subtly and unconsciously concretize our understanding of ourselves as gendered, racialized, or as national citizens. Sociologist Rebecca Coleman shows how, in consumer culture, teen girls concretize themselves as young women via images of women's and girls' bodies (Coleman 2012). This process is iterative and relational; it re-activates every time a woman or girl brushes against images that speak to her unconscious understanding of herself or others. In this sense, becoming can be considered both a material and ideal process of constituting ways of being. It brings together bodies, images, or other active entities in the world. Under the framework of becoming, then, authenticity is no longer located within the body of one given individual but continuously constituted through active material interactions with the world—similar to Charles Taylor's ethics of authenticity mentioned earlier (1992). Importantly, one can become something 'other' than what is typically configured by hegemonic or dominant algorithmic logics by embracing or being embraced by heterogeneous elements and flows—in short, by interrupting the algorithmic process. According to this view, broader power formations always impose modes of being, sometimes violently through

15 Speaking more broadly, Deleuze and Guattari define becoming as a process and experience of change, bifurcation, transformation, and critically, mobility (Deleuze 1997). Most critically, here one is not a single being, but rather composed of multiplicity of elements and traversed by heterogeneous flows. The "subject" and "object" as separate entities does not work here; rather, active entities like humans can be thought of as assemblages with moving parts, constantly under exchange and reconfiguration.

systemic discrimination and criminalization, and at other times by inviting us to identify and solidify ourselves with specific subject positions (to self-identify as algorithmic inputs). Many radical or transformative authors (i.e., Preciado 2018) thus conceive of "becoming" as a political practice that refuses dominant definitions and modes of existence and instead embraces ways of being that rewrite dominant social forms such as the nuclear family, heterosexuality, or whiteness.

In response to questions of gender, sexuality, labor and commodification, scholars have discussed the commodification of authentic emotional intimacy. Elizabeth Bernstein explains that sex work in San Francisco increasingly entails selling an erotic experience premised upon the performance of authentic interpersonal connection (Bernstein 2007). Sex workers become "girlfriends for hire," revealing much about the cultural expectations of sexuality, political economy, and desire. While Bernstein tracks authenticity, desire, and sexuality, Jane Ward's *Not Gay: Sex Between Straight White Men* investigates what constitutes authentic sexual orientation (Ward 2015). While clandestine and fleeting moments of sexuality happen between men who identify as straight, these acts are coded as achieving alternative ends or as being "necessary," revealing that notions of authentic sexuality depends as much on dominant social narratives as it does bodily urges. Ward argues that sex via these rituals of hyper-masculinity and whiteness (for example, frat parties and initiations) preserve a sense of authenticity and reliability that supports heterosexuality.

The onset of digitality has both disrupted and amplified the work of categories, sex, and gender. The radical feminist collective VNS Matrix first coined the term cyberfeminism in 1991 in their manifesto of the same name, continuing that "we are the future cunt" (Matrix 1991). Linking to and moving beyond essentialist schools of feminist thought rooted in biological difference, VNS Matrix and subsequent cyberfeminists follow the work of feminist philosophers like Haraway and Braidotti in portraying digital femininity as fundamentally changed by technical prostheses (Haraway 1990; Braidotti 2011). Hegemonic codings of authenticity are challenged by cyberfeminism in its commitments to destabilizing norms of internet culture founded in patriarchal capitalism.

Queer and Trans Theory, and the Valence of Failure

Extending but distinct from feminist theory, both Queer and Transgender theory promote more egalitarian forms of life and the flourishing of a queer, non-determinate authenticity by challenging dominant norms for gender and bodies. They disrupt normal and normative ways to "authenticate" humanness (Allen and Mendez 2018). Specifically, these theories oppose the notion of biological womanhood as authentic womanhood and thus feminisms that base collective action on the idea that all women share natural and/or essential qualities. They argue that these feminisms, which exclude trans and non-normative bodies, rely too deeply on concepts of motherhood, and thus maintain hetero-patriarchal systems that naturalize hierarchy and subjection (Hester 2018).

Queer theory addresses the limits of such categories and their associated access to power (see, especially, Gowlett and Rasmussen 2014). Queer and trans theory operationalize the concept of queerness, queer-bodies, and techno-humanism as an alternative base for feminist and radically egalitarian action; they seek to produce activist affinities by reworking concepts of kinship (making affinities) and coalition (Haraway 1991; Puar 2013). The building of affinity-based rather than identity-based coalitions to oppose hetero-capitalist conditions is a key goal of Donna Haraway's (1990) famous "Manifesto for Cyborgs," which has become a wellspring for post-humanist, feminist, socialist, and queer and trans theory. In this sense, queer and trans theory expands past studies of sexuality and humanist activisms and reconsiders what constitutes not only the queer and/or post-human body (Haraway 1990) but also queer space and queer life in context of the heteronormative state (Berlant and Warner 1998; Delany 1999).

"Queerness" as a fluid, indefinite term seeks to rework power relations by unsettling common and essentialist understandings of identity, gender, and sexuality. For example, queer theorist Jenny Sundén compares gender to technologies: fragile, unstable machinery prone to breakage and breakdowns and needing continuous maintenance, upgrades, and reboots (which produce the illusion of organic wholeness, naturalness, or transparency, as we may perceive new technology) (Sundén 2015). Similarly, queer theorist Annamarie Jagose describes queerness as the fluid becoming of entities, during which ongoing relations with other actants (whether molecules, doctors, or peers) constitute humans and nonhumans (Jagose 1996). Given this, the school of thought dubbed "New Materialism" echoes queer theory in how it takes agency not as fixed within actors but as a "dynamism" emerging from the intra-active relations between active or passive entities (Barad 2007). Theories of new materialism can thus act as "queering tools" (Allen and Mendez 2018), disrupting the authentication of a biological, "natural," or instinctive human essence.[16]

Alongside this deconstruction, queer theory explores non-heteronormative, non-patriarchal, and anti-statist forms of being that queer the way we think about, relate to, and organize ourselves. Queer theorist Paul B. Preciado, for example, presents countersexuality as the end of a naturalist ethos that legitimates the subjection of others (Preciado 2018). Like communications scholar Helen Hester's xenofeminism (Hester 2018), Preciado posits

16 Comparing queer theory to new materialism helps describe the deconstructive element of Queer theory; such makes familiar or taken-for-granted concepts strange, unfamiliar, and draws attention to systems or "technologies" (Preciado 2018; Foucault 1988) of power that make formations like heteronormativity and binary bodies seem natural (Dinshaw 1995).

that (what count as) sex organs and sexuality are complex biopolitical technologies. When used within performative acts, these technologies concretize a heterosexual order that promotes sex for procreation and for the perpetuation of the nuclear family unit, which underlie capitalist social reproduction. Preciado's call for re-scripting the body through performative acts and modes of being evokes Haraway's conception of bodies as "not ending at the skin, but rather as coming to exist through their relation and involvements with other humans and non-humans, creating posthuman, technological assemblages" (Haraway 1990). With these anti-normative bodies and/as technologies, Hester argues, new worlds that refuse alienation and that nourish queer existence can be generated (2018).

Debates over the body and its radical queering mark a gulf between queer and trans theorists, specifically over how to maintain the radical potential of "queering," while still advocating the validity of the existence and genders of trans people (Elliot 2010). Queer theorist Jack Halberstam argues that trans persons should remain unintelligible to avoid incorporation into mainstream systems of power via binary or fixed gender systems (Halberstam 2011). In contrast, transgender theorist Susan Stryker posits that "transgender" increasingly functions as the site in which to contain all gender trouble within queer theory, "thereby helping secure both homosexuality and heterosexuality as stable and normative categories of personhood" (Stryker 2004). This speaks to queer theorist Jasbir Puar's concept of homonationalism, which describes how the state recognizes some forms of (productive, white) queerness (e.g., the legalization of gay marriage, or the acceptance of trans people in the American military) to pacify activisms against imperial state violence towards Black and Brown bodies (Puar 2013). Others question what queer theory's emphasis on fluidity means for folks who embrace more conventional gender or identity categories (Martin 1994; Namaste 1996). The key rifts in this literature reflect divergences in theoretical and political concerns, in disciplinary allegiances, and in discourses of gender and sexuality. At stake in these debates is whether the knowledge and the material conditions needed to secure the well-being of transgendered persons will be fostered or undermined, and what it means to support trans-gendered persons while still enacting radical ways of being.

These ways of being unsettle normative hetero-sexing technologies of the state and the body and, in turn, destabilize the algorithms of the hegemony that determine what it means to be an authentic body, being, and subject of the state. As the next chapter shows, this unsettling emerges through performances—through both identification and nonidentification, performance allows for disruptions of the flow of algorithmic formatting.

[4]

Performing Authenticity

While authenticity is relational at its core, the power to judge and assign it as a trait underlies hegemonic projects across the globe. Potential resistance emerges through the ability to reclaim the audience for whom authenticity is performed. While identity and its determinations underlie the political power of authenticity to judge and permit, performance is required for these judgments to occur (and re-occur). Performance, then, is key to authenticity—both in its appearance across culture and the ways that it mediates these appearances.

Across disciplines, researchers explain authenticity through performance. Viewing authenticity through the lens of performance and theatre studies moves away from performance as metaphor to performance as theatrical practice. It investigates the impact of audience perception, acting, repetition, liveness and markets on authenticity, by starting with performance studies scholar Richard Schechner's influential definition of performance as both a "showing doing" and "twice-behaved behaviors" (2017, 28). This broad and general definition—covering everything from performing arts to sports, reality TV to politics, religious rituals to cultural production—presumes two things. The first is the existence of an audience ("showing doing"). The second is the temporal necessity of repetition ("twice-behaved behaviors"). Together, these two elements highlight how authenticity *becomes* algorithmic, and likewise illustrate how digital cultural trends like social media microcelebrity are part and parcel of the acceleration of algorithmic authenticity. The "audience," in this metaphor, is the datum upon which authenticity is algorithmized: as always relational, any performance of authenticity takes in both the actant and the audience in its calculation. But it does not reveal itself as algorithmic solely through this calculation, instead emerging through the "twice-behaved behaviors" of the performance itself. Remember that algorithms are "iterable and repeatable rulesets". The "twice-behaved" nature of performance implies its repeatability. A performance, then, acts to glue together audience and actant in the expression of their being-together, and its iterability implies its algorithmic nature. The performance lens offers a means to answer just how it is that things gain the gloss of the authentic (and thus the true), outside of judgments of facticity: performances, affects, and expressions. Yet at the same time, for an act to appear authentic, the audience must also be ignored (or at least acted as if it is). In common understandings of authenticity, explicitly doing something for or because of an audience renders an act theatrical and thus inauthentic.

Authenticity: Acting "As If"...

Performance requires an audience. This does not mean that the doer/performer and the spectator must be together at the same time and space; rather that the act of "showing" implies a viewer who will witness the action/doing. At the same time, the audience must usually be ignored for an act to appear authentic: explicitly doing something *for* or *because* of an audience renders an act theatrical and thus inauthentic. This anti-theatrical prejudice is particularly evident in art history. Art critic and historian Michael

Fried distinguishes "the authentic art of our time" from "other work which, whatever the dedication, passion and intelligence of its creators, seems to me ... corrupted or perverted by theatre" (Fried 1967). This does not mean that the mere presence of a beholder/audience makes art authentic—art and performance, after all, are meant to be seen—rather that self-consciousness does. Drawing from the work of philosopher Denis Diderot, Fried describes painting in France from the mid-1750s to 1781 as exemplifying authentic art because viewers of the paintings are treated as though they are not there (Fried 1989, 5). Even as Fried derides "theatrical" work—work that acknowledges the presence of an audience—as inauthentic, a theatrical "as if" grounds authenticity, for Fried's authentic subject (artwork) acts *as if* there were no beholder/audience.

Fried's discussion of theater and theatricality has nothing to do with the art form and medium called theater; it has to do with painting, sculpture, and their audiences. If one takes medium specificity seriously and considers the actual conditions of Western theater, we see more clearly how pretense—the "as if"—grounds the so-called anti-theatrical. The actor, conscious of the audience, pretends that the spectators are not there, denying any "consciousness of being beheld" (Fried 1989). Diderot describes the ideal actor who embodies this relationship as having "in himself an unmoved and disinterested onlooker" and as playing "from the head," "from calculation," not "from the heart" or "from nature" (Diderot 1883, 14, 16, 28). This ideal actor reproduces and generates—*without experiencing themselves*—intense emotions in an audience. For this to be possible, the emotion must be given "a definite course" (Diderot 1883, 64), and there must be "a beginning, middle and an end." These are the predefined rules that shape what performance can be. In other words, they are the algorithms of performance.[1]

1 In acting, the crafting of authenticity goes hand in hand with the revelation and/or production of the self. According to theater artist Joseph Chaikin, "[a]cting is a demonstration of the self with or without a disguise" (Chaikin

 Not all follow Diderot's definition of authentic performance as successful reproduction *without experience of* emotion. The psychological conception of naturalistic performance, for example, takes the written character as the grounds for understanding performance. This means that an actor's performance is effective insofar as they can "tap into the authentic emotions of the characters" (Pavis 2016, 18). This mode of performance still disavows the presence of the audience and its influence. More recent experimental theater, however, undermines "the idea of the actor prevalent in the mimetic and psychological tradition ... as actors take pleasure in showing how their roles are crafted, built up, an effect of trickery, and in deconstructing

[1972] 1980, 2). While there are vast differences amongst various acting traditions and methods of demonstrating the self, the presence of the self as a conduit to truth in performance remains. Considering this, the showing of the/a self always lies behind "showing doing," and the (assessment of the) authenticity of the performance hangs on the skill in the revelation of the self. As performance scholar Philip Auslander notes: "We often praise acting by calling it 'honest' or 'self-revelatory', truthful; when we feel we have glimpsed some aspect of the actor's psyche through her performance, we applaud the actor for 'taking risks' or 'exposing herself'" (Auslander 2002, 53). At stake in the manufacturing of authenticity in the realm of acting is the difference between good and bad acting, and emotion—or the lack thereof—plays an important part in distinguishing between the two. For theater director-designer and theorist Edward Gordon Craig, for instance, it is the very subjectivity of the actor—his/her/their vanity, self-display, and subjection to whimsical emotions—that is at the root of bad acting. To rid the actor of these faults and the theater of bad acting, Craig advocated for the replacement of the human actor with an "Über-marionette" (1957). In a different direction, influential director and theorist Konstantin Stanislavski—the progenitor of the infamous "method" mode of acting—rooted the authentic display of the self in the actor's capacity to emote and devised a "technologizing process of producing emotion" to aid the actor in this endeavor (Torn 2011, 6). This process aims to enable "good acting," which "is the result of 'intuition' and 'inspiration', where actors forget themselves and start spontaneously 'living a part', reacting freely and without self-consciousness to the dramatic situation as if it were a unique and contingent event" (3). Authenticity, which relies on affective labor, thus "is the ultimate product of postmodern capitalism, and the most pervasive means for producing authenticity in our world remains Stanislavski's 'magic if'" (5-6).

their own so-called authenticity" (ibid.). Such a theatrical display acknowledges that authenticity is always artificial and constructed, and this knowledge grounds the audience's enjoyment. Furthermore, these understandings allow for the role of dialogic media, from news anchorship to social media confessionals, to be understood as performative despite their apparent displays of authenticity. While there exists an apparent full presentation of the self, this presentation is influenced by the fact that the relationship between actor and audience is always mediated. Such an assumption implies that mediation alters, on some fundamental level, the very possibility of authentic expression—in other words, mediation makes up part of the algorithmic process that results in authenticity.

Emotion also plays an important role in naturalist evaluations of a performance's authenticity. Authentic performance is that which appears "natural or genuine," while the inauthentic "feels faked, forced, or imitative" (Henderson and Gabora 2013, 2524). "Feels" is crucial here. The more emotionally intense something is, the more authentic it is felt to be. Trilling explicitly connects authenticity with intense emotion, pointing to "the violent meanings in the word 'authentic' and its root etymology" (Trilling 1972, 131). The extremity, however, is not limited to violence: "nowadays our sense of what authenticity means involves a degree of rough concreteness or of extremity" (ibid., 94). As further developed in other sections, this insight gains renewed relevance in the present-day media context where "extreme" speech in online platforms appears authentic because it transgresses the codified mores of political correctness, and where authentic media often transgress rather than maintain the fourth wall.

Liveness, Repetition, and Refusal

The "twice-behaved behaviors" in Schechner's definition of performance brings to the fore questions regarding the relationship between performance, liveness and authenticity, and the relation between the original and the copy. According to Peggy Phelan, "[p]erformance's only life is in the present;" it "cannot be saved, recorded, documented, or otherwise participate in the circulation of representations of representations: once it does so it becomes something other than performance" (Phelan 1993). This tenuous relationship with time and historical presence "plunges" live performances into visibility, making it disappear into memory "and the unconscious where it eludes regulation and control" (ibid., 146). Given the vanishing nature of live performance, any repetition will inevitably have to be an altogether different performance and any copy is inauthentic. Because the time over which a performance occurs "will not be repeated," argues Phelan, the repetition of a performance marks its uniqueness.

Against Phelan, who stresses the immediacy of the now and the disappearance of performance "into the realm of invisibility" (Phelan 1993, 148), performance studies scholar Rebecca Schneider argues that performance remains and that any present moment is necessarily "syncopated"—shot through with other moments in time. Syncopated time challenges the modern notion of linear time, since the "'sedimented acts' that comprise the social are already a matter of [Schechner's] 'twice-behaved behavior'" (Schneider 2011, 92). Because the past exists through the present (repetition presumes a past occurrence), there can be no such thing as a pure, immediate, present moment. The past not only remains, but influences certain actions and behaviors, "rather like a prompt, a script, an instruction, or a 'training manual'" (Schneider 2011, 45). Schneider further describes authenticity as haunted by "the threat of the imposter status of the copy, the double, the mimetic, the second, the surrogate, the feminine, or the queer" (2011, 47).[2]

2 Writing specifically about Civil War reenactments, Schneider notes that "any drive to 'authenticity'" ("an idealized time," "an authenticity that should have been, according to the reenactors' interpretations") "will automatically be vexed, necessarily including strained and awkward attempts at

This notion of a script or an algorithm is crucial to understanding debates surrounding authenticity and performance, for the scripted nature of performance puts it at odds with authenticity construed as spontaneous and "real." In televisual liveness, media scholar Alla Gadassik tells us, "(failed) performance"—performance that seemingly fails to stick to a given script—helps generate "effects of presence and authenticity" (Gadassik 2010, 118).[3] The "live broadcast" promises a privileged access to the unrepeatable, the unstaged, the unprogrammed. What happens in "real time" appears untampered—thus the privileging of surveillance footage within fictional film as "real" (Levin 2002). Gadassik argues that this promise relies on "the possibility that anything could happen, that real events or accidents could break through the carefully managed stream of information" (2010, 118). Notably, this view implies that the perception (or impression) of authenticity depends on the existence of a script or program—for how can there be an interruption of a "controlled flow" (program) if there was no programming (scriptedness) to begin with?

In a very different manner, researchers have also linked the breaking, contestation, or refusal of dominant scripts, which uphold colonial, extractive, heteronormative, white supremacist formations, to forms of artistic resistance. Focusing on the work of queer performers of color such as Marga Gomez, Jean-Michel Basquiat, Isaac Julien, Richard Fung, Vaginal Davis, Ela Troyano, Carmelita Tropicana, Pedro Zamora, and Felix Gonzalez-Torres,

mimesis—such as blackface minstrel routines in the camp among white reenactors [...] or women cross-dressing as male soldiers" (2011, 55).

3 In the context of television, authenticity thus emerges through "'unscripted' affective moments, when words fail and something else breaks through: gasps, pauses, tears, silences, aggressive eruptions" (Gadassik 2010, 118). This applies to different kinds of television genres. Sociologist Laura Grindstaff, for instance, writes about talk shows whose perceived authenticity rests on the "concrete, physical evidence of real, raw emotion" (Grindstaff 2002, 116), the display of which is encouraged by the TV hosts (and thus is, in a way, pre-scripted or algorithmic—its possibilities are bound by the initial moment).

performance studies scholar José Esteban Muñoz centers queer self-making and world-making through practices of disidentification that undermine "notions of authenticity and realness" (Muñoz 1999). Neither assimilation nor strict opposition to hegemony, disidentification remakes and rewrites a dominant script in order to work "on and against dominant ideology" (ibid., 11). By repeating racist and homophobic images and stereotypes *with difference,* these practices "offer the minoritarian subject a space to situate itself in history and seize social agency" (1).[4] Repetition with difference performs what media scholars Lilian Mengesha and Lakshmi Padmanabhan call a refusal of reproduction, which disrupts the binary of assimilationist or strictly oppositional modes of sublimated existence, as well as what philosopher Édouard Glissant calls the totalitarian desire for "roots" (Mengesha and Padmanabhan 2019; Glissant 1997).[5] Performance, thus, both grounds and undermines the construct of authenticity. As theorist Jon McKenzie has argued, it is a double-edged sword, reinforcing oppressive systems and containing the possibility of resistance and transformational change (2001, 30).

Reality TV

4 For Muñoz, strategies of "iteration and reiteration" ground the (counter) performativity of disidentificatory performance and "build worlds" (Muñoz 1999, 196). Residing both within the present and the future and "insisting on the minoritarian subject's status as world-historical entity … the temporality of disidentificatory performance disrupts the mandates of the 'burden of liveness'," which "labours to relegate the minoritarian subject to the live and the present and thus evacuates such personages from history" (198).

5 The essays that Mengesha and Padmanabhan curate for the "Performing Refusal/Refusing to Perform" issue of the journal *Women & Performance* (2019) center refusal understood as "precisely those tactics of illegibility, opacity, and inaction, that remain outside of the field of political action properly conceived" (Mengesha and Padmanabhan 2019). The focus here is on "performative modes of non-productivity and non-reproductivity" that "challenge the episteme of performance as dependent on repetition," bringing us back to Schechner's "twice-behaved behaviors."

Readers might be noticing a theme—performance reveals the inherent contradictions of authenticity. Nowhere are these better revealed than reality television and its claims to capture and present documentary evidence of real humans experiencing real emotions and interactions. The reality of reality TV, however, is that it is highly formatted and edited: production teams often script or wireframe particular interactions; video editing can alter the chronology, effect, or significance of recorded events; and contestants in competitions can work with predetermined results before the season even starts shooting. Each episode follows the same plot as does each season. Their surprises and "off-script" moments are tightly edited to follow the same trajectory. As media theorist Wendy Hui Kyong Chun has argued, reality TV is algorithmic: a program, in all senses of that word (Chun 2016).[6]

To cover over its algorithmic nature, reality TV registers its authenticity through supposedly transgressive moments, "moments when participants' composure breaks down, when their gestures or interviews betray their emotional states" (Gadassik 2010, 126). To feel authentic, however, such moments can't appear forced or staged. What happens, then, is that the very integrity of the self's control over their own appearance is challenged: as Gadassik notes, "contestants are often submitted to extreme physical exhaustion or supplied with large quantities of alcohol," to break down the measured or considered presentation and performance of the self (Gadassik 2010, 126). Built on the cult of "the amateur," reality TV exploits its contestants both financially and psychically, sublimating the view of the

6 As software pioneers Herman H. Goldstine and John von Neumann explained in the early days of electronic computers, programming is "the technique of providing a dynamic background to control the automatic evolution of a meaning" (Goldstine and von Neumann 1951). The term "automatic" here may seem questionable, but the Greek root *autos* ("self") embedded in this term links "automatic" to "authenticity," "authority," and "authorship." To be "automatic" is to be self-generating, whether as human or machine.

 amateur or non-elite as a means toward class liberation into the media machinery of class exploitation.

The narratives of reality TV become "dramas of authenticity." They are "unprecedented demonstrations of emotionality" or "displays of intensity." But these displays are always aimed towards the audience, and the presentation of contestants' supposed inner emotional life is designed to overcome the distance between the viewer and the viewed. Analyzing group behaviors at public memorials, sociologist E. Doyle McCarthy argues that authenticity is central to collective agency—it forms the basis for participation (McCarthy 2009). Similarly, in *Reality TV: the Work of Being Watched*, Mark Andrejevic illustrates how reality TV's claims to represent real life, alongside its interactive elements, create a stronger bond than average entertainment (Andrejevic 2004).[7] But since the authenticity of contestants is coerced, authority over the self and its presentation belongs not to the contestant but the producer. The authenticity of the reality TV situation is constructed and enacted by the producer according to a particular set of technical rules—and this power illustrates not

7 According to Andrejevic, reality TV audiences are set up to believe that they are sharing in the labor of reality TV's happenings and production (Andrejevic 2004). With interactivity built into many reality shows, from audience voting to interactions with stars on social media, the audience is set up not as a passive observer of media content, but as co-producers of the culture that they're consuming alongside the contestants. This level of interactivity creates a closer bond between audiences and the show itself, whether the labor of the audience really plays out—there's no notice, for example, of KPMG auditing American Idol results. The perception of the production process as a shared labor activity, both on part of the audience as participants in their interactivity as well as the "real people" within the program, gives a false promise of de-alienating labor, structured around "real" content for "real" audiences. The nature of reality programming seeming unscripted, less predictable, and therefore less mediated, play a key role in seeing it as a "real," authentic form. Participants on the show offer "real" emotions, making themselves visible for all to see.

only what counts as authentic, but mediates the very options of presenting authenticity.[8]

It is premature to attribute these differing levels of the "authentic" performance solely to reality TV: the differing media environments upon which performances are enacted have a much longer history in mainstream Western culture. Take the Hollywood "star." The star is someone whose very real processes of growing up and living life are documented through a separate stream of media from the performative roles they take. The dual existence of their public life and their characters in popular culture means that the star exists less as role or individual but somewhere in the middle, what Christine Glendhill calls the "star-image" (Gledhill 1991). The boundaries between the star's real life and their performative representation split into what Meyers calls the "authentic" celebrity and the "real" celebrity. The former is the star known for what they do performatively and appear within; the latter the life of the star outside of these public performances (Meyers 2009). Each narrative of the authentic performance is, then, contextualized and co-opted by the

8 Biressi and Nunn similarly look at how the authenticity of reality TV is linked to a wider understanding of "therapeutic culture" and emotional realism (Biressi and Nunn 2005). The new economies of realism make use of confession, exhibitionism, and emotional revelation as key indicators of authenticity and an ethical commitment to the audiences. Reality TV audiences gauge authenticity or truthfulness of shows based on their level of emotional realism and personal motivation. Disclosure in confessional television plays a key role in whether a show is "authentic"—often portrayed through individuals speaking directly to the camera—indicating a lack of mediating presence and a switch of power relations. Confessions and disclosure work to construct a publicly recognized and authenticated persona, feeding into what Zizek describes as the authentic 20th-century passion to penetrate the Real Thing (Žižek 2008, 12). Reality TV offers a new realism where authenticity is marked by an individual's self-revelation and interactions with others. But visibility is necessary, as authenticity is judged by viewing or seeing. Confessions need to be declamatory and within a public forum. Reality TV is thus "real" insofar as we view these candid processes of identification and voyeurism, accessing the personal through a multi-perspectival vantage point.

"metanarrative" of the celebrity's life unfolding outside the performance. This merges the appearances over image and sound technologies: the live performance or stage show, the music video, or the magazine cover. This play between performance and "real"ness complicates the idea of authenticity. It leads to the creation of what Goodwin calls the "star-text," an inscription in popular culture where characterization, fiction, and narrative exist "at the point of narration, outside the diegesis of individual songs, live performances, or video clips, through the persona" of the star (Goodwin 1992, 103).

Goodwin, along with other cultural studies critics of the mid-80s and 90s (see, e.g., Grossberg 1986) understand metanarrative as the means by which pop culture industries influence public taste. Metanarratives draw together the "authentic" and the "real" celebrity life into a singular image, wherein the content of each narrative plays into each other. And through this, the use-value of the given performance as commodity increases: the appeal of the performance extends beyond its content, becoming a part of the construction of the metanarrative in which audiences have invested time, energy, and affective attachment (Buxton 1983). Star-images become, then, "particularly potent ideological symbols," able to "stand in for our needs and desires within modern society" (Meyers 2009).

Cultural Production

Reality TV's dramas of authenticity rely on an extra level of mediation added to the star-image, a sort of make-believe version of witnessing reality unfold. As the genre gained popularity, its patterns began to permeate throughout mainstream culture, especially through its melting of the fourth wall. Cinematic fictional metanarratives like "franchises" or "cinematic universes," alongside the entrance of "intellectual property" into common parlance, reflect the shift of this relationship between performative authenticity and audiences. This interplay between the "real" and the *real*, the variety of mediated levels upon which performances are judged and audiences are created, has evolved from reality TV towards the level of media properties themselves.

Contemporary studio mega-mergers both horizontal (on the level of human, creative, and performative capital) and vertical (on the level of streaming infrastructures and production pipelines) provide a shared reality that grounds the perception of authenticity. While Disney, for example, has always been involved in the production of star-images (think of the "Mickey Mouse Club" and its incubation of preteen Hollywood stars), the company's maneuvers in the past decade—purchasing the intellectual property rights of major media franchises in order to release sequels, merchandise, and various tie-in cultural items—work towards a greater level of control in the creation and maintenance of textual and narrative coherency across a variety of mediums (Kunz 2007; Holt 2011). The difference between the narrative mediums of the individual star and the studio boils down to how they integrate into the shared commercial atmosphere: while the star's metanarrative construction occurs on their own terms, it occurs within the media of others. In contrast, the construction of Disney's *Star Wars* universe or its *Marvel* Cinematic Universe place the powers of narrative construction beyond the single studio picture towards one that encompasses both the fictional and the material, from in-house streaming television shows to toys to tie-ins. On the level of mass capital, the metanarrative production system ends up relating to the same questions raised under the guise of performativity, liveness in time, and authenticity raised earlier in the chapter: cultural products and different intellectual properties act "as-if" the contingencies of their individual narratives bind them together, as opposed to the strategic designs of the corporations and companies who own them.

Despite its scale, the question of the commodification of culture is not a new one, nor is it restricted to the strategies of intellectual property claimants. Theodor Adorno's famous essay, "On Jazz," critiques the popular music of his time as an aural mimicking of the processes of industrial capital (Adorno [1936] 1990). This mimicry is embodied through a common set of maneuvers to engineer sonic pleasure on the level of the content itself. Ruled by the rhythmic principles of "syncopation" and a "simultaneity of excess and rigidity" (45, 46), Adorno posits that popular music neutered the political and liberatory potentials for art by appealing to shallow feelings of entertainment. This divorces authentic understanding of the self's position in society from their experience of culture as shaped by the symbolic desires of capital, flattening experience through the rhythmic and lowest-common-denominator appeal of mechanically optimized music.

The initial appearance of this same-ness via industrial production marks cultural fields as spaces of contention in the question of authenticity. These contentions result in the emergence of subcultures, positioned directly in contrast to mainstream hegemony. Dick Hebdige, in his seminal 1981 work *Subculture: The Meaning of Style*, defines *style* as the mode against which subcultures understand both their own principles and their oppositional status to hegemonic culture (Hebdige 2012). Style, as Hebdige has it, is the act of reappropriating previously mundane items to give them meaning. By reading culture as a set of techniques of ascribing meaning to objects and symbols, the subcultural reappropriation of the forgotten is an "act of refusal" (2). This expression of "forbidden contents in forbidden ways" (92) fosters communication between group members, and conceptions of authentic belonging are built through this shared identity and refusal. Authenticity emerges through the binary that style constructs, creating an "us" and "them" dichotomy through which the "us" becomes authentically identified through specific style.

The "us" and the "them" of subcultural authenticity is maintained through the construction of taste (Thornton 1996). The same hierarchies of taste that paint the dominant modes of culture in the mainstream are likewise constructed within the subcultural arena, levels based on a form of capital premised on "hipness" that Thornton dubs subcultural capital. The process of authenticating subcultural legitimacy is predicated on the acquisition and maintenance of subcultural capital through signs and style. The ensuing value hierarchy influences the operational characteristics of a subculture, from who decides which sign becomes a style, to who members look to for recognition. This ultimately lends itself to how the acquisition or embodiment of this style ratifies a person as authentic to the community.

In *Profane Culture*, Willis continues Thornton's analytic of taste towards the idea of "realness" as constituting the material conditions upon which taste's meting out of subcultural capital lies (Willis 2014). Authenticity, from Willis' perspective, is understood through relations to style such as music taste or ways of living that attempt to cultivate a direct expression of a unique self. And since these groups are formed through their attachment to these expressions of style as reactions to the mainstream, these tastes and expressions are inherently performative. Through the construction of "profane materials" as style (5), Willis posits a "dialectic of cultural life" wherein only the "real people" at work on "real objects" are those who produce new movements in style, through play and distortion of cultural objects (2).[9]

This dialectic helps us understand what, and how, different points in time yield the same phenomena as differently "subcultural" yet algorithmic in their emergence. In the 1960s, for example, rock music began to take on a posture of "sincerity" that granted it special status as the soundtrack of rebellion (Grossberg 1986). By positioning itself against mainstream music, it took back the mantle of "authenticity" previously associated with blues, jazz, and other genres. As the liberatory political spirit in these genres

9 Groups appear to present a subcultural form of resistance to capitalist media and commercialism through their cultivation of alternative identities and sense of self. Authenticity, from Willis' perspective, is understood through relations to style such as musical taste or ways of living that cultivate a direct expression of a unique self.

was slowly overtaken by the institutional politics and modes of production discussed above by Adorno, rock's aesthetic performance of difference allowed it to differentiate itself (Frith and Goodwin 2004, 1).

Yet as quickly as it emerged, rock music mutated as its more traditional bearers became subject to the same sort of mass commercialization it initially resisted. One such mutation was the evolution into 1970s punk, whose own genre innovations (the wholesale minimization of the distance between performer and audience) adopted markers of intimacy and authenticity that opposed the larger-than-life spectacle presence of rock. Bands dressed like audience members; songs were made up of simple and unskilled instrumental performances; performers played on risers or on the same floor on which the audience stood as opposed to the removed and distant performance stage (Strong 2016). But punk's influence waned as record labels began to understand and co-opt the production of these markers of authenticity (Barker and Taylor 2007); as Hebdige noted specifically, because punk's conceptual base was founded upon a "ruptur[ing]" of mainstream bourgeois culture, it was always susceptible to being co-opted because it took these very patterns into consideration (Hebdige 2012).

From the ashes of this rupture came the grunge movement in the late 1980s and early 1990s. Instead of growing out of punk's sideways glance at mass culture—Malcolm McLaren, the manager for notorious U.K. punk band the Sex Pistols, once described the band as a "French situationist"-style project (Reynolds, 2010)—grunge began as an underground movement tied to a single label, the Seattle-based Sub Pop. The music was a distorted, heavier, and slower-paced counterpart to punk's fast-paced vocal shouts, while its iconic style of tattered flannel shirts and oversized thrifted clothes fostered a winking "sartorial irony" that deterritorialized the Ivy-league brands that donned the labels (Le Zotte 2017). Grunge took the countercultural ethos of rock and punk beyond the aesthetic level, incorporating an activist political bent to its culture ("anticorporate DIY punk, feminist and queer politics" as Moore puts it (2004, xx)). This move to incorporate the political into the music's subculture made visible the conditions of its production, fostering "a sense of authenticity and sincerity" (116) that it shared with punk's performative intimacy. It also served to flip the script on what had at that point been a half-century of the reverse incorporation of music into mainstream capitalist means of production.

But the suicide of Nirvana lead singer Kurt Cobain at the height of the band (and the movement's) fame began to spell grunge's end, including a subsumption into mass culture and corporatization. Just as punk's firm tongue in cheek gave way to grunge's sincerely affected cynicism, so too had capital grown up proper and understood how to provide for cultural and social needs, by subsuming alternative subcultures and cultural production into the commodity market. The musical and political scenes that flourished in the late 1980s "scattered across the American landscape" and from their very start opposed "to corporate capitalism" and "the culture industry," soon became the "central component in a developing form of creative capitalism that valorized its sincerity of expression and idiosyncrasy of style" (Moore 2004, 120). Thus, the commodification of grunge signaled the last cries of the notion of "anticommercial authenticity," as it became "more and more difficult to maintain the familiar opposition between bohemia, on the one hand, and mass culture, rationalized workplaces, and state bureaucracy" (121).[10]

10 What remains, then, for the pop-cultural connoisseur searching for an authentic connection through cultural entertainment? How to get around the question of capital's intrusion on "authentic" culture when that very authenticity is historically tied so tightly to being against capital? Well, one could evade the question in a sense through professional wrestling. Wrestling has never been the image of authenticity—but it's never tried to be. As Roland Barthes observes, "the public is completely uninterested in knowing whether the [wrestling] contest is rigged or not ... it abandons itself to the primary virtue of the spectacle" (Barthes 1972, 25). This is, in one way, the opposite of what grunge and punk imagined themselves to

 Importantly, this narrative of the gradual overcoming of subculture by capitalism has been challenged by cultural critic Tiziana Terranova and many others. According to Terranova, capitalism does not "appropriate anything," for capitalism is the

be: the purity of spectacle, not in reaction-to any sense of mass culture but responding with an outsized version thereof. By forming itself around the spectacle, wrestling wears its status as production on its sleeve. And while its "fakeness" often leads to dismissal from any serious consideration of cultural valuation (Sehmby 2002), this very fakeness can tell us much about the tensions between the capitalization of cultural production and the role that metanarrative plays in it. Central to Western wrestling entertainment companies like the WWE is the concept of *kayfabe*. Like the concept it describes, kayfabe itself is a notoriously slippery thing to define: Herrman calls it "the agreement among wrestlers not to disclose to outsiders that wrestling matches are staged fights" (Herrmann 2016 xx); Assael and Mooneyham call it the "metaphor for (wrestlers') wall of silence" (Assael and Mooneyham 2004); in recent times, as the kayfabe became a known fact of wrestling entertainment, audiences no longer required "even a thin veneer of realism" (Weinstein 2011), and kayfabe has now become a part of the multiple articulations of reality and performance that occur in the wrestling universe. To "break kayfabe" is to go off-script during a match; to pierce the veil of illusion of the performance. This is but one means of real or "authentic" events entering the scripted narrative universe of wrestling. In the "Montreal screwjob" of 1997, WWE mastermind Vince McMahon Jr. began a chain of kayfabe eruption when he went off-script as ring announcer to claim that wrestler Bret Hart had submitted—despite the scripted agreement that the contest would end in a draw. Hart spat on McMahon and gave him a black eye (Assael and Mooneyham 2004). But the next week, McMahon spun these events into the narrative of the story—setting up what would become the increasingly porous wall between kayfabe and its breaking that has since characterized the WWE, with events now incorporating the internal workings of the wrestling *business* and unscripted events being spun into the live stage performance. Insofar as this question of the cultural image is concerned, Baudrillard's description of the simulacra as the characteristic aesthetic mode of contemporary capitalism—the substitution of representational modes for the real thing—is the best model through which to understand wrestling (Baudrillard 1994). And unlike the cultural movements subject to capital co-option, or the metanarrative as a means of combining disparate media forms, wrestling illustrates a different understanding of authenticity under performance—one that acknowledges its performative nature not as a lie to always struggle against, but inherent to any potential art in itself.

field from which culture itself now flows. Far be it to alienate its cultural producers, contemporary capital is deeply dependent on nurturing, exploiting, and exhausting the "cultural and affective production" of its labor force (Terranova 2004, 94). Cultural objects are not created outside of capital and then subsumed, but emerge from "a complex history where the relation between labor and capital is mutually constitutive, entangled and crucially forged" (ibid.). Affect becomes production itself by positioning consciousness as what the philosopher Bernard Stiegler calls a "metamarket" (2014, 16), where marketing and media technologies manufacture the very desires that drive action itself according to a set of algorithmic rules. Yet the very fact that this positioning can never be complete allows for a renewed importance on what Terranova calls "immaterial labor," the productive activities of knowledgeable consumers. As she puts it, "neither capital nor living labor want a labor force that is permanently excluded from the possibilities of immaterial labor. But this is where their desires stop from coinciding. Capital wants to retain control over the unfolding of these virtualities and the processes of valorization" (42).

(Fine) Art

Struggles against capitalist subsumption characterize contemporary art because artists and artwork are commonly thought to represent a more "authentic" mode of communication and engagement with the public, particularly when they move beyond traditional gallery or museum contexts. For example, art critic Nicolas Bourriaud (2002) describes the 1990s turn towards interactive encounters and experiences as democratizing the experience of art, for this "relational aesthetics" allows the audience to engage with and contribute to the work itself actively and authentically. To incorporate the unpredictable—namely, the element of the viewer's experience and affect—disrupts the algorithmic chain that determine the development of commodified art. However, art critic Claire Bishop notes that participatory art often shorthands authentic experience (2012). She cautions that viewing collaborative art as inherently pro-social, ethical, and "good" prevents an honest and critical assessment of it, because doing so makes the perceived authentic connection with its audience the only metric that matters. This, in turn, frames this type of artwork as escaping the neoliberal artistic enterprise on which it fundamentally rests.

Yet—like punk and grunge's attempts to cancel out their own subsumption by incorporating audience experience—participatory art and its "authentic connection" has been taken up in corporate contexts (Martorella 1990; Rectanus 2002; Wu 2003; Stallabrass 2004). Instead of escaping the algorithmic construction of authenticity, participatory art's "authenticity" becomes the very thing corporatized. Examining Facebook's use of artists and artwork in both its internal and external public relations efforts, media scholar Fred Turner outlines how these artists are portrayed by Facebook as "free" and "authentic," with no acknowledgement of how they and their work are being used for a corporate agenda (2018). He argues that corporations use the presence of artwork in their facilities to signal their open-mindedness and liberal thinking.

Media studies scholar Sarah Banet-Weiser similarly discusses street art, its projection of authenticity, and the ways in which that projection is used by corporate hegemony (Banet-Weiser 2012). Because street art positions itself as the "anti-brand," it is used to make the "creative city" seem more authentic to its residents—and it helps residents imagine their neighborhood as unique (116). Artists, seeing their works' successes in these contexts, then adapt their practices to the demands of branding and marketing. In both instances, the "creative" serves as a shorthand for the authentic—a presumably unfiltered aesthetic experience that somehow bucks or subverts the status quo, while at the same time being shaped, guided, and used by the ostensibly inauthentic systems it supposedly rejects. This veneer of authenticity allows powerful interests to utilize supposedly countercultural or anti-establishment artwork in their favor and enables them to adopt its qualities into their own hegemonic practices.

Digital Identity

Questions of authenticity and performance thus become attempts to appear as the former while hiding the latter. These questions are amplified within and by digital space and its complicated relationship to "real life." The emergence of the internet and its new modes of communication offered a new lens for performativity and identity. As internet usage became mainstream via seemingly anonymous chat rooms, bulletin boards, and listservs, researchers began to investigate how identity and digitality mutually shaped each other. Questions abounded about how digital freedom could enable more authenticity than the offline world—and much critical work pushed back on this by revealing how technical worlds are not divorced from social ones (see, e.g., Nakamura 1995; Chun 2016).

Internet studies researcher Lisa Nakamura's ethnographic analysis of the MMORPG and chat space LambdaMOO shows how the 1990s internet encouraged the use of stereotyped racialized identities, while also discouraging the use of everyday racialized identities (1995). The idea of the "stereotype" to emulate illustrates another aspect of authenticity's algorithmic nature: stereotypes, as culturally established representations, invoke a script of performativity. And without the material identifiers of the stereotyped group (such as in digital space), it becomes a performable and performative identity. This emerged on LambdaMOO when participants "passed" as others in ways that adhere to "authentic" racial stereotypes. When describing their characters as racial tropes, players enact what Nakamura calls an "orientalized theatricality": a form of identity tourism, where these typically white characters can enjoy a temporary appropriation of what they conceptualize as a stereotyped racialized character.

 As the internet evolved to produce visual game-worlds and massively multiplayer online spaces, other anthropological and sociological studies of internet life emerged. Anthropologist Tom Boellstorff's extensive digital ethnography on Second Life expanded concepts of authentic online identity and authentic cultural worlds by examining the forms of cultural life and ritual, social interaction, and self-constitution that occurred within the Second Life digital world (Boellstorff 2008). Second Life's wholesale virtualization of identity gives us a glimpse into social media and its performance of identity as the stuff of digital life.

The move to make the online and offline coincide buttresses the economic model of social media sites like Facebook. Throughout the 2000s, corporations like Google insisted that the verification of transparent, authentic online identities was the surest means of promoting safety and combating online aggression (Chun 2016), even though considerable aggression and cyberbullying comes from non-strangers; for example, from the "friends" in Facebook networks (111-113). This notion of the familiar, or the authenticated friend as *safe,* and the stranger as non-trustworthy *enemy* organizes the construction of for-profit digital networks. "Real Name" policies enable profitable data mining operations and profiling, which has ushered in a new era of advertising, hyper-curated to the online self. As information scholars Oliver L. Haimson and Anna Lauren Hoffman have shown, the forceful insistence by social media companies on verified identities as authentic proves harmful to marginalized individuals with fluid or non-normative identities (Haimson and Hoffmann 2016). Media studies scholar Harris Kornstein elaborates further on this in their analysis of the #mynameis campaign, which was initiated by drag queens to resist the "real-name" requirement from Facebook in order to use their performing name, and therefore make themselves more discoverable for, amongst other benefits, generating income-leads (2020). #mynameis also highlights the importance of reputation, branding and authenticity to branding, micro-celebrity and the digitally edited self.

Social media as a stage for identity highlights the dual nature of performance and its role in authenticity. Feminist scholar Terri Senft first defined micro-celebrity in her study of Internet camgirls as "a new style of online performance that involves people 'amping up' their popularity over the Web" (2008, 25). Subsequently, micro-celebrity has been considered a practice, identity, attitude, strategy, and form of labor—and sometimes all of these at once. It typically implies some degree of success as well: the status of being famous to a small number of people. These contingencies place the "authenticity" of the microcelebrity at the forefront. As Alice Marwick writes, "becoming a micro-celebrity requires creating a persona, producing content, and strategically appealing to online fans by being 'authentic'" (2013, 114). Micro-celebrities are expected to be more "authentic" than Hollywood celebrities, presumably because they are outside of the star-making industry (119). This reflexive positioning against the well-established patterns of the Hollywood star-making machine sets up a particular set of scripts and behaviors that dictate the format, genre, and tropes of microcelebrity. Self-branders, however, reveal their authenticity not simply by disclosing inner secrets, but rather by "being measured against an ideal of honesty, in that the information that is revealed has a constancy." (121). The authentic microcelebrity "discloses in the name of knowledge production, and the authentic self of self-branding is one that edits in the name of knowledge consistency" (207). Marwick's insight here is that micro-celebrity authenticity is a functional matter—it is a process that mediates the (intimate) knowledge required for the relationship of authenticity to develop. This algorithmic process takes the self-image of the authentic person as its input and puts forth the image of the authentic, (supposedly) unmediated celebrity as its output.

Algorithmic authenticity in micro-celebrity practices of self-branding, however, is far from straightforward. It is deeply contextual, relational, tenuous, and fragile. Audience perceptions of authenticity are, moreover, highly susceptible to variations in even the smallest details of a performance like the emotional valence of a post or the audience's degree of interaction with content online (Luoma-Aho et. al. 2019). Cunningham and Craig describe the emergence of social media influencer culture as "previously amateur creators" who begin "professionalizing" towards content innovation and the incubation of their own media brands (2017, 71). The cultures surrounding microcelebrity and social media influencers are likewise directly tied to the market, especially after Google's purchase of YouTube in 2006 introduced direct lines of "monetization" for content. But they also exceed the capacity for building community of those brands tied to major professional companies in their grounding of the culture in the seemingly personal relationship between audiences and the microcelebrity. This results in what Horton and Wohl called the "para-social interaction" of mediated direct addresses to audiences (1956), where feelings of "intimacy and familiarity" offer an affective tie that covers up the market deliberations that go into constructing these networks (Marwick 2015, 348). Horton and Wohl constructed their definition based on the intimacies crafted through talk-television shows and the idea of "welcoming in" the character onto the screen into one's living room. Marwick likewise notes the role that these technical infrastructures play in the cultivation of authenticity: "the visible, comparable metrics of social media success ... encourages the active inculcation of an audience," metrics which play into an "online attention economy in which pageviews and clicks are synonymous with success" (347).

Reputation and Branding

But the question of these parasocial relationships and authenticity are not so clear-cut as to be the sole result of these attention economies. There is a complicated balance between brand cultures and the perception of authenticity, especially as brand cultures congregate around the microcelebrity. The "parasocial" relationship appears as more authentic through its contrast with the authenticity played into by abstracted brands, alongside the way that it calls an audience into being through the "intense interactivity" supported by social media platform infrastructures (Cunningham & Craig 74). And while the question of branding hangs over the cultivation of influencer status, this "only enter[s] the picture after the establishment of this dialogic relationship between authenticity and community" (ibid., 74).

Rebecca Lewis observes the immediacy of this dialogic relationship as part and parcel of the explosion of what she calls the reactionary politics of micro-celebrity (2020). The lack of mediation between influencers and fanbases has supported the growth of political content created by "citizen journalists" who leverage the perception of authenticity that arises in the contrast between microcelebrity and mainstream branding. Taken up as a part of the growth of digitally native right-wing communities commonly referred to as the "alt-right," these practices of micro-celebrity become the means by which "mainstream media [and] social justice-driven politics" are given implicit association in the minds of viewers. By performing this parallel, the mainstream media is positioned as the realm of the inauthentic while these right-wing "citizen journalists" become the source of unmediated truth, and likewise their reactionary politics the seemingly authentic alternative to the social justice concerns of the mainstream.

Thus, the digitally edited self acts as the groundswell for contemporary information economies and their attempts to profile, capture, and trade in the digital traces of real existence. All kinds of personal information are routinely collected and collated online, and this has given rise to a new economy of reputation in which one's value—such as one's sense of oneself and self-worth and one's economic and financial standing—are produced via algorithms and digital networks. Reputation covers many modes of authenticity, from user authentication to how one builds a sense of authentic self. The new reputation economies make surveillance a pre-requisite for publicity, economic opportunities, and legal recognition (Noble 2018).

The rise of reputation as form of capital, as communications scholar Alison Hearn tells us, is the latest in a long line of attempts by market capitalism to commodify all relations (Hearn 2017). In this system of capital, one's identity—rather than one's labor power—matters, and to survive and stay relevant, one must engage in a constant process of self-management and promotion. That is, in a reputation economy, one becomes a brand. Brands, as media studies scholar Celia Lury argues, are the logos of the global economy. They organize economic, cultural and social activities; they establish patterns of exchange; and they act as economic, social and cultural contracts (Lury 2004). Branding seeks to create "trustworthy" connections between producers to consumers. The successful brand goes beyond economic trust-worthiness to express cultural values and shared imaginaries. Attachment to brands is therefore deeply affective and not just limited to socio-economic standing, so much so that branded products are seen as more authentic than similar counterparts.[11]

11 Within this discussion, it is also important to acknowledge and consider the historical power imbalances involved with cultural appropriation in the context of authenticity. Cultural appropriation itself is frequently framed as taking pieces of a culture from outside of one's own experience, but the act involves specifically taking elements of a culture from marginalized and often exploited groups (Arya 2021). These issues, particularly in racialized forms, can be seen in advertisements, which often appropriate cultural language while erasing cultural meanings or individuals behind them (Roth-Gordon, Harris, and Zamora 2020). These instances of performative authenticity through cultural appropriation often invite stereotyping as a means of creating cultural shortcuts to profit (Grazian 2010). The commodification of culture and identity involves power dynamics and the emphasis on authenticity as a means of achieving capital. Cultural appropriation and the commodification of culture are also inextricably linked to one another (Arya 2021). Dominant culture uses elements of marginalized groups and cultures for their aesthetics, producing a circumstance where purchasing

In exceeding simple commodification, brands elide the "crass realm of the market"—they rely on the interplay between audience and object and enact the commodification of the participatory experience discussed above. Branding, Sarah Banet-Weiser tells us, "has extended beyond a business model"; it is now "both reliant on, and reflective of, our most basic social and cultural relations" (2012, 4). Brands are the stuff of a consumerism that is about much more than selling and acquiring products for their use; they "invoke the experience associated with a company or product," a "story told to the consumer" that, when successful, "becomes a story that is familiar, intimate, personal, a story with a unique history" (4). They create what cultural critic Raymond Williams calls "structures of feeling," spaces in which individuals feel safe, secure, relevant and authentic (Williams 2011). Marketing—the set of techniques that construct brands—establish *how* something can be of value for consumers. But because of the basic fictions involved in branding's stories, marketing mobilizes authenticity in a paradoxical way. To establish value, one needs not only to understand but also foster needs and wants: a successful product must be perceived as an authentic answer to some problem. It therefore must tap into not only material needs but also affective, social and emotional desires. Under capitalism, the problem is that marketing not only uncovers but also actively transforms and shapes needs and wants according to logics of ever-expanding profits, so that consumerism gets equated with happiness and freedom. The Frankfurt School denounced this as a "false consciousness" at play in branding; cultural industries attempt to translate emotions, relations, connections and so on into material and immaterial commodities to be purchased and configure a different conscious relationship to the market and the affective support provided and perpetuated by brands (Marcuse [1964] 1991).

power becomes an important part of this form of cultural exploitation (ibid.).

Identifying with a brand "impacts the way we understand who we are, how we organize ourselves in the world, what stories we tell ourselves about ourselves" (Banet-Weiser 2012, 5). By leveraging and attempting to reproduce the experiences and affects that make up our own conception of the self, then, brands become "symbolic structures for crafting selves, creativity, politics, and spirituality" arising directly from the organization of cultural meaning by economic exchange (5, 6). They become how authenticity is constructed and performed. In this way, they are the focal point of the subsumption of past cultural movements' attempts to escape or elide the construction of the self as consumer. But branding authenticity is not simply cynical. The stereotypical yearn for an "authentic past" doesn't hold up to much scrutiny—it's unlikely that most people would rather forage for food, construct their own shelters, and live close to the land, saying nothing about this type of nostalgia's links to racist and supremacist thought. Instead of this yearning, Banet-Weiser makes a point of stressing the deep ambivalence of contemporary brand cultures: there is no rigid difference between having and selling an authentic experience, since all sectors are increasingly commodified. Even though brand cultures often reduce politics to an individual issue, they still function as places for communal connection. The brand's desire *to* reflect, adopt, and stand-in as representations of the self means that the brand relationship is co-constitutive, moving outward from the individual's wants: they work to make one become "more of who you are" and "who you were meant to be" (2012, 8). They remain a locus of intimacy, built upon "the accumulation of memories, emotions, personal narratives and expectations" (Banet-Weiser 2012, 9).[12] Self-branders are thus told that their personal brand is

12 This latter point emphasizes how brands can be seen as "authentic" or in possession of a "moral purpose;" branding entails "the making and selling of immaterial things—feelings and affects, personalities and values—rather than actual goods" (Banet-Weiser 2012, 7). This accumulation of "memories, personal narratives, and expectations" is the result of the transformation of cultural labor into capitalist business practices (8), and this culture becomes

"a perception or emotion, maintained by somebody other than you, that describes the total experience of having a relationship with you" (McNally and Speak 2011, 4).

Branding authenticity amplifies authenticity as a form of self/subject possession–as Wendy Hui Kyong Chun notes, branding creates the dictum wherein "through your authenticity, I become authentic; and through my identification, you become authentic" (Chun 2021, 148). Self-branders are told that, to be authentic to themselves, they must be authentic to others (Marwick 2017, 80). This authenticity requires a transparent self *to be seen as branded*, because the self of the self-brand must be immediately perceived and perceptible; it grounds recognition. Therefore, visibly transgressing conventions—revealing what would otherwise be considered "odd" or risqué characteristics—is the easiest way to be recognized as authentic.

The ambivalence of this programmed and constructed visibility makes authenticity appear hard to define, but easy to identify. As a commentator writing for *Forbes* Magazine during the election put it: "like beauty, pornography, and soul, it is hard to define authenticity. As Supreme Court Justice Byron White noted, 'you just know it when you see it'" (Zogby 2016). This notion of authenticity as immediately recognizable—and as resisting any formulaic attempts to mimic it—is linked to the notion of authenticity as "real" or "true." But again, this feeling of "realness" depends on an investment that emerges spontaneously from a considered, crafted, formulaic and algorithmic set of conditions, then performed for an audience whose role is to validate and authenticate the very conception of the internally emergent self.

subject to the logic of exchange in how its constant making and remaking depends on the relationship between individuals and a system of production. Thus, brand cultures feel more "real" than the outputs of capitalism past, in that they become an integral part of the symbolic structures of culture that support the split of what is seen as authentic versus what is not.

Conclusion

The growing connection of our everyday experiences of the "real" world to networks, relations, techniques, and groups that each have their own way of judging the authentic threatens to overtake our own capacities. Not only is the question of authenticity a question about what is real, it is about how this judgment itself is determined. Not simply either/or, the authentic is that which is "in accordance with fact," something that "accurately reflect[s] a model." It is a "truthful correspondence," an "accurate reflection." Thus, authenticity is not simply the question of being true, nor of appearing as such: it is about the ways that these two things intersect, and how these intersections—sometimes explicit, sometimes latent—shape our social behaviors, conflicts, and fabrics. Authenticity, therefore, is not a characteristic of a thing in the same way that a color, or a mathematical equivalence, may be. It is not a sensorial or analytic judgment. It is instead a question of how particular characteristics that are self-evident intersect and combine to set the basis upon which the concerns of our social reality and conceptions of truth take form.

But under the increasingly algorithmic management of life, this vision itself can fall apart. Mediated representations of authenticity reflect their subjects' performances back onto them, encouraging reiterating behavior that divorces experience from the ability to judge the authentic. The drive to political individuality that fuels the search for the "authentic" self sets up its subjects to follow similar paths and adopt the same set of behavioral patterns to discover this supposedly entirely unique situation. Identity politics becomes "inauthentic" and "noncollaborative" and solidarity becomes "disingenuous." These systems, in other words, presume neoliberalism: that the world is filled with competing individual agents and that to act collectively—to make conscious collaborative connections with others—is to "game" the system. These "collaborative" programs thus reveal that, even though authenticity and creativity may depend on communal relations, they are everywhere treated as individual attributes, and authenticity is reduced to "authentication": the demand that users act "genuinely" so that they can be better pigeonholed into collectively determined "latent" categories.

The algorithmic repetition of authenticity reduces it to "sincerity": to be "genuine" is to be consistent—without intention or design. This transparency is sold as a way to free and protect the user. With this so-called transparency—with "user authentication"—we have not only seen an explosion of e-commerce, but also a blossoming of cyberbullying and cyberporn. Further, the use of "unique identifiers" as a proxy for transparent screens has enabled big data analytics. The data gathered by the U.S. National Security Agency are so valuable precisely because private corporations have been pushing "unique identifiers" to track users across time and space, without which it would be difficult if not impossible for them to create "neighborhoods." Recommender systems cannot easily function without a way of reliably tracking users or items across time or space. They also cannot function without the ability to group and cluster users—who do not act like unique snowflakes, but rather array themselves like iron filings before poles that both draw them together and repel them from each other.

Thus the individual borne out of the idealization of authenticity looks increasingly like the result of an algorithm, shaped by the world they live in and following its schematics when the "authentic" self as isolated self is pursued. The output of algorithmic authenticity is not the "authentic" self as isolated self, but one that is always contradictory, always running from those social determinations (truth, facticity) that set the stage for defining authenticity in the first place. Yet this is not to say that authenticity and facticity coincide. The latter is fickle, contingent, and not always visible; the former, almost always, wins out, because what is true and what is true to me depends on who, where, and what I am.

Contemporary "post-truth" is better understood when we look at these factors. The supposedly neutral and objective ground used in fact-checking is much more contested than it seems, and the relations that make up what we see as authentic are the ground for truth not as emergent from fact but trust. This very patterning becomes the condition for trust's emergence. While the dictum "to thine own self be true" motivates a host of behaviors, "thine own self" must express a truth to indeed be true to. And as we know from those who study the history of establishing truth, it is always informed by its milieu. The algorithmic appearance and management of authenticity that has been traced through this book comes full circle, pre-empting its own designs.

Whither truth, then, when verification loses its value? Such is the question that this book has attempted to (set up an) answer to. To get there, and to continue questioning, we have moved through the algorithmic flows through which we have already been input. This book has attempted to catalyze the answer by exploring the centrality of authenticity to questions of the real and the true. In turn, it responds to the contemporary question of the viral spread of mis- and disinformation. Taken as a whole, it has attempted to reveal that verification and fact-checking are necessary but not sufficient to tell apart what is fictional and what is factual, and what is in turn perceived as authentic. To address "fake news," we must continue to address questions of ideology, infrastructures, data circulation, economics, media strategies and the formation of identities and groups (Figueira and Oliveira, 2017).

Authenticity supplements behavioralist models of users—which presume that users are marionettes or lab rats—controlled by social media (Orlowski et al. 2020). As researchers have shown, social media users craft personas online with public / social engagement in mind (D. Boyd 2014; Duguay 2017; Enli 2015, 2017; Gilpin, Palazzolo, and Brody 2010). Performance grounds identity in ways that are neither cynical nor insincere (Goffman 2007; Butler 1997). We don't end, then, simply with research questions, but a proposal for a means of answering them. The performance-based schema in table 1 attempts to bring together the book's various investigations into a way to diagnose, pinpoint, and explore the ramifications of authenticity.

Code	Description
Algorithmic scripts	How actions are captured and scripted through user profiling and algorithmic recommendations systems, among others.
Character development	What sequence and modes of expression are allowed by the platforms and enacted by users and bots.
Performance	Creating personas and provoking real-time interactions, both online and offline.
Mise-en-scène	The multi-platform environment, location of the screen, devices and third parties.
Genre	The types of affect and the goal of the interactions (advertising, etc.).
Audience / networks	How the user is clustered and who s/he is exposed to.
Seriality	How links/recommendations/breadcrumbs lead users along certain trajectories.
Advertising / Marketing/ Economics	How advertising and marketing models fuel outrage and click-bait, and click/like farming.

Table 1: Prototype schema for countering and/or reducing the spread of mis/dis-information and viral junk content circulation.

To understand the impact of authenticity, we need to understand how these categories interact. We need to understand the implications of users as characters in that drama we so wantingly call social (media). Thinking through our roles as characters does not diminish our authenticity. It moves us away from dubious allegations of our era as "post-truth" and endless accusations of "fake news." It lets us approach an answer to "why and how—under what circumstances (social, cultural, technical and political)—do people find information to be true or authentic?" It enables us to build systems that acknowledge collective action and intentional actions as "good" rather than "malevolent."

These performances, especially online, are not solitary but rather collectively formed and scripted. New media relentless emphasize *you*: *You*tube.com; what's on *your* mind?; *You* are the Person of the year. New media are n(*you*) media, but this *you* is never simply singular, but also plural—*you* is a particularly shifty shifter in English. This singular plurality forms the basis for data analytics, which treats individuals "like" others. Big Data—in its most popular current form as a glorified form of network analytics, used by corporations such as Netflix, Target, and FICO—mines our data not simply to identify who we are (this, given our cookies and our tendency to customize our machines is very easy), but to identify us in relation to others "like us." Our scripts, our lines, are constantly impacted by the actions and words of others, whom we are constantly correlated with and unconsciously collaborate with.

Most hopefully, focusing on authenticity thus moves us away from endless debates over whether something is real—to prolonging crises in the name of knowledge—and towards engaging outcomes, motivations and effects.

References

Adorno, Theodor W. [1936] 1990. "On Jazz." *Discourse* 12 (1): 45–69.

Ahmed, Sara. 2007. "A Phenomenology of Whiteness." *Feminist Theory* 8 (2): 149–68. https://doi.org/10.1177/1464700107078139.

———. 2014. *The Cultural Politics of Emotion*. Second edition. Edinburgh: Edinburgh University Press.

Allen, Samuel H., and Shawn N. Mendez. 2018. "Hegemonic Heteronormativity: Toward a New Era of Queer Family Theory." *Journal of Family Theory & Review* 10 (1): 70–86. https://doi.org/10.1111/jftr.12241.

Alonso, Ana María. 2004. "Conforming disconformity: "Mestizaje," hybridity, and the aesthetics of Mexican nationalism." *Cultural Anthropology* 19 (4): 459–90. https://doi.org/10.1525/can.2004.19.4.459.

Andrejevic, Mark. 2004. *Reality TV: The Work of Being Watched*. Lanham, MD: Rowman & Littlefield Publishers.

Anzaldúa, Gloria. 1999. *Borderlands*. San Francisco: Aunt Lute Books.

Arendt, Hannah. 2014. *On Revolution*. Edited by Jonathan Schell. New York: Penguin Books.

"Authenticity, n." n.d. *OED Online*. Oxford University Press.

Baldwin, James. 1965. "The White Man's Guilt." *Ebony*, August, 47–48.

Bair, Madeleine. 2012. "Is It Authentic? When Citizens and Soldiers Document War." *WITNESS Blog*. https://blog.witness.org/2012/11/is-it-authentic-when-citizens-and-soldiers-document-war/.

Banet-Weiser, Sarah. 2012. *Authentic: Politics and Ambivalence in a Brand Culture*. New York: New York University Press.

Barker, Hugh, and Yuval Taylor. 2007. *Faking It: The Quest for Authenticity in Popular Music*. 1st ed. New York: W. W. Norton.

Barker, Joanne. 2011. *Native Acts: Law, Recognition, and Cultural Authenticity*. Durham: Duke University Press.

Barstow, David, Susanne Craig, and Russ Buettner. 2018. "Trump Engaged in Suspect Tax Schemes as He Reaped Riches From His Father." *The New York Times*, October 2.

Barthes, Roland. 1981. *Camera lucida: reflections on photography*. 1st American ed. New York: Hill and Wang.

Baym, Geoffrey. 2005. "The Daily Show: Discursive Integration and the Reinvention of Political Journalism." *Political Communication* 22 (3): 259–76. https://doi.org/10.1080/10584600591006492.

Beauvoir, Simone de. 2011. *The Second Sex*. 1st Vintage Books ed. New York: Vintage Books.

Bellinger, John B., and Vijay M. Padmanabhan. 2011. "Detention Operations in Contemporary Conflicts: Four Challenges for The Geneva Conventions and Other Existing Law." *American Journal of International Law* 105 (2): 201–43. https://doi.org/10.5305/amerjintelaw.105.2.0201.

Beltrán, Cristina. 2009. "Going Public: Hannah Arendt, Immigrant Action, and the Space of Appearance." *Political Theory* 37 (5): 595–622. https://doi.org/10.1177/0090591709340134.

———. 2015. "Undocumented, Unafraid, and Unapologetic: DREAM Activists, Immigrant Politics, and the Queering of Democracy." In *From Voice to Influence: Understanding Citizenship in a Digital Age*, edited by Danielle Allen and Jennifer S. Light, 80–104. Chicago, IL: University of Chicago Press.

Berlant, Lauren. 2006. "Cruel Optimism." *Differences* 17 (3): 20–36. https://doi.org/10.1215/10407391-2006-009.

Berlant, Lauren, and Michael Warner. 1998. "Sex in Public." *Critical Inquiry* 24 (2): 547–66.

Berlin, Isaiah. 2002. *Liberty: Incorporating Four Essays on Liberty.* Edited by Henry Hardy and Ian Harris. Oxford: Oxford University Press.

Berman, Marshall. 2009. *The Politics of Authenticity: Radical Individualism and the Emergence of Modern Society.* New ed. London; New York: Verso.

Bernays, Edward L. 1928. "Manipulating Public Opinion: The Why and The How." *American Journal of Sociology* 33 (6): 958–71. https://doi.org/10.1086/214599.

Bernstein, Elizabeth. 2007. *Temporarily Yours: Intimacy, Authenticity, and the Commerce of Sex.* Chicago: University of Chicago Press.

Bonilla-Silva, Eduardo. [2003] 2018. *Racism Without Racists: Color-Blind Racism and the Persistence of Racial Inequality in the United States.* Fifth ed. Lanham: Rowman & Littlefield Publishers.

Bounegru, Liliana, Jonathan Gray, Tommaso Venturini, and Michele Mauri. 2018. "A Field Guide to 'Fake News' and Other Information Disorders." *SSRN Electronic Journal.* https://doi.org/10.2139/ssrn.3097666.

Boyd, Colin, Anish Mathuria, and Douglas Stebila. 2020. *Protocols for Authentication and Key Establishment.* Routledge. https://doi.org/10.1007/978-3-662-58146-9.

Braidotti, Rosi. 2011. *Nomadic Subjects: Embodiment and Sexual Difference in Contemporary Feminist Theory.* New York: Columbia University Press.

Brock, André L. 2019. *Distributed Blackness: African American Cybercultures.* New York: New York University Press.

Brown, Elspeth H. 2005. *The Corporate Eye: Photography and the Rationalization of American Commercial Culture, 1884-1929.* Baltimore: Johns Hopkins University Press.

Bucher, Taina. 2006. "Want to Be on the Top? Algorithmic Power and the Threat of Invisibility on Facebook." In *New Media, Old Media: A History and Theory Reader*, edited by Thomas Keenan and Wendy Hui Kyong Chun, 1–16. New York: Routledge.

Bullynck, Maarten. 2016. "Histories of Algorithms: Past, Present and Future." *Historia Mathematica* 43 (3): 332–41. https://doi.org/10.1016/j.hm.2015.07.002.

Buolamwini, Joy, and Timnit Gebru. 2018. "Gender Shades: Intersectional Accuracy Disparities in Commercial Gender Classification." *Proceedings of Machine Learning Research* 81: 1-15.

Burton, Anthony G. 2022. "Blackpill Science: Involuntary Celibacy, Rational Technique, and Economic Existence Under Neoliberalism." *Canadian Journal of Communication* 47 (4). https://doi.org/10.3138/cjc.2022-07-25.

———, and Dimitri Koehorst. 2020. 'The Spread of Political Misinformation on Online Subcultural Platforms'. *Harvard Kennedy School Misinformation Review*, September. https://doi.org/10.37016/mr-2020-40.

Butler, Judith. 1988. "Performative Acts and Gender Constitution: An Essay in Phenomenology and Feminist Theory." *Theatre Journal* 40 (4): 519–31. https://doi.org/10.2307/3207893.

———. 2006. *Gender Trouble: Feminism and the Subversion of Identity*. New York: Routledge.

Buxton, D. 1983. "Rock Music, the Star-System and the Rise of Consumerism." *Télos* 1983 (57): 93–106. https://doi.org/10.3817/0983057093.

Byrd, Jodi A. 2011. *The Transit of Empire: Indigenous Critiques of Colonialism*. Minneapolis: University of Minnesota Press.

———. 2014. "Tribal 2.0: Digital Natives, Political Players, and the Power of Stories." *Studies in American Indian Literatures* 26 (2): 55–64. https://doi.org/10.5250/studamerindilite.26.2.0055.

Callon, Michel. 1984. "Some Elements of a Sociology of Translation: Domestication of the Scallops and the Fishermen of St Brieuc Bay." *The Sociological Review* 32 (S1): 196–233. https://doi.org/10.1111/j.1467-954X.1984.tb00113.x.

Campolo, Alexander, and Kate Crawford. 2020. "Enchanted Determinism: Power without Responsibility in Artificial Intelligence." *Engaging Science, Technology, and Society* 6 (January): 1–19. https://doi.org/10.17351/ests2020.277.

Chaplin, Charles. 1936. *Modern Times*. United States: United Artists.

Cheng, Anne Anlin. 2001. *The Melancholy of Race: Psychoanalysis, Assimilation and Hidden Grief*. Oxford: Oxford University Press.

Chun, Wendy Hui Kyong. 2016. *Updating to Remain the Same: Habitual New Media*. Cambridge, MA: The MIT Press.

———. 2021. *Discriminating Data: Correlation, Neighborhoods, and the New Politics of Recognition*. Cambridge, MA: The MIT Press.

Coleman, Rebecca. 2012. *The Becoming of Bodies: Girls, Images, Experience*. Illustrated edition. New York: Manchester University Press.

Coulthard, Glen Sean. 2014. *Red Skin, White Masks: Rejecting the Colonial Politics of Recognition*. Minneapolis: University of Minnesota Press.

Cunningham, Stuart, and David Craig. 2017. "Being 'Really Real' on YouTube: Authenticity, Community and Brand Culture in Social Media Entertainment." *Media International Australia* 164 (1): 71–81. https://doi.org/10.1177/1329878X17709098.

Crawford, Kate. 2021. *Atlas of AI*. New Haven: Yale University Press.

Daly, Mary. 1999. *Quintessence...Realizing the Archaic Future: A Radical Elemental Feminist Manifesto*. Boston: Beacon Press.

Darnton, Robert. 2017. "The True History of Fake News." *The New York Review of Books*, February.

Daston, Lorraine. 1995. "The Moral Economy of Science." *Osiris* 10: 2–24.

——, and Peter Galison. 1992. "The Image of Objectivity." *Representations* 40: 81–128. https://doi.org/10.2307/2928741.

Dean, Jodi. 2005. "Communicative Capitalism: Circulation and the Foreclosure of Politics." *Cultural Politics* 1 (1): 51–74.

De León, Jason. 2015. *The Land of Open Graves: Living and Dying on the Migrant Trail*. Oakland, CA: University of California Press.

Delany, Samuel R. 1999. *Times Square Red, Times Square Blue*. New York: New York University Press.

Desrosières, Alain. 1998. *The Politics of Large Numbers: A History of Statistical Reasoning*. Cambridge, MA: Harvard University Press.

Didion, Joan. 2008. *Slouching Towards Bethlehem: Essays*. New York: Farrar, Straus and Giroux.

Digital Democracies Institute. 2022. "Beyond Verification: Authenticity and Mis/Dis-information." https://digitaldemocracies.org/research/beyond-verification/.

Donovan, Joan, and danah boyd. 2018. "The Case for Quarantining Extremist Ideas." *The Guardian*, June. https://www.theguardian.com/commentisfree/2018/jun/01/extremist-ideas-media-coverage-kkk.

DuBois, W. E. B. [1903] 2007. *The Souls of Black Folk*. Edited by Brent Hayes Edwards. Oxford; New York: Oxford University Press.

Drucker, Johanna. 2011. "Humanities Approaches to Graphical Display." *Digital Humanities Quarterly* 005 (1).

Dyde, Sean. 2015. "George Combe and Common Sense." *The British Journal for the History of Science* 48 (2): 233–59. https://doi.org/10.1017/S0007087414000922.

Einwiller, Sabine A., and Sora Kim. 2020. "How Online Content Providers Moderate User-Generated Content to Prevent Harmful Online Communication: An Analysis of Policies and Their Implementation." *Policy & Internet* 12 (2): 184–206. https://doi.org/10.1002/poi3.239.

Elliot, Patricia. 2010. *Debates in Transgender, Queer, and Feminist Theory: Contested Sites*. Farnham, Surrey, England; Burlington, VT: Ashgate Publishing.

Eng, David L., and Shinhee Han. 2019. *Racial Melancholia, Racial Dissociation: On the Social and Psychic Lives of Asian Americans*. Durham: Duke University Press.

Fanon, Frantz. [1967] 2008. *Black Skin, White Masks*. New ed. London: Pluto Press.

Farkas, Johan, and Jannick Schou. 2018. "Fake News as a Floating Signifier: Hegemony, Antagonism and the Politics of Falsehood." *Javnost - The Public* 25 (3): 298–314. https://doi.org/10.1080/13183222.2018.1463047.

Favor, J. Martin. 1999. *Authentic Blackness: The Folk in the New Negro Renaissance*. Durham: Duke University Press.

Ferrara, Alessandro. 1993. *Modernity and Authenticity: A Study of the Social and Ethical Thought of Jean-Jacques Rousseau*. Albany, NY: State University of New York Press.

Figueira, Álvaro, and Luciana Oliveira. 2017. "The Current State of Fake News: Challenges and Opportunities." *Procedia Computer Science*, CENTERIS/ProjMAN/HCist 2017, 121 (January): 817–25. https://doi.org/10.1016/j.procs.2017.11.106.

Finn, Ed. 2017. *What Algorithms Want: Imagination in the Age of Computing*. Cambridge, MA: The MIT Press.

Fleming, Peter. 2009. *Authenticity and the Cultural Politics of Work: New Forms of Informal Control*. Oxford: Oxford University Press. https://doi.org/10.1093/acprof:oso/9780199547159.001.0001.

Fraser, Nancy. 2014. *Justice Interruptus: Critical Reflections on the "Postsocialist" Condition*. Hoboken: Taylor and Francis.

Fraser, Nancy, and Axel Honneth. 2003. *Redistribution or Recognition? A Political-Philosophical Exchange*. London; New York: Verso.

Fried, Michael. 1967. "Art and Objecthood." *Artforum*, Summer.

Frith, Simon, and Andrew Goodwin. 2004. *On Record: Rock, Pop, and the Written Word*. London; New York: Routledge.

Fromm, Erich. 1984. *The Fear of Freedom*. London: Ark Paperbacks.

Gadassik, Alla. 2010. "At a Loss for Words: Televisual Liveness and Corporeal Interruption." *Journal of Dramatic Theory and Criticism* 24 (2): 117–34.

Gardner, William L., Claudia C. Cogliser, Kelly M. Davis, and Matthew P. Dickens. 2011. "Authentic Leadership: A Review of the Literature and Research Agenda." *The Leadership Quarterly* 22 (6): 1120–45. https://doi.org/10.1016/j.leaqua.2011.09.007.

Gray, Jonathan, Carolin Gerlitz, and Liliana Bounegru. 2018. "Data Infrastructure Literacy." *Big Data & Society* 5 (2). https://doi.org/10.1177/2053951718786316.

Gillespie, Tarleton. 2014. "The Relevance of Algorithms." In *Media Technologies*, edited by Tarleton Gillespie, Pablo J. Boczkowski, and Kirsten A. Foot, 167–94. Cambridge, MA: The MIT Press. https://doi.org/10.7551/mitpress/9780262525374.003.0009.

Gledhill, Christine, ed. 1991. *Stardom: Industry of Desire*. London; New York: Routledge.

Goffman, Erving. 2007. *The Presentation of Self in Everyday Life*. London: Penguin Books.

Golomb, Jacob. 2012. *In Search of Authenticity: Existentialism from Kierkegaard to Camus*. Hoboken: Taylor and Francis.

Goodwin, Andrew. 1992. "Metanarratives of Stardom and Identity." In *Dancing in the Distraction Factory: Music Television and Popular Culture*, 98–130. Minneapolis: University of Minnesota Press.

Gover, Angela R., Shannon B. Harper, and Lynn Langton. 2020. "Anti-Asian Hate Crime During the COVID-19 Pandemic: Exploring the Reproduction of Inequality." *American Journal of Criminal Justice*, July, 1–21. https://doi.org/10.1007/s12103-020-09545-1.

Gowlett, Christina, and Mary Louise Rasmussen. 2014. "The Cultural Politics of Queer Theory in Education Research." *Discourse: Studies in the Cultural Politics of Education* 35 (3): 331–34. https://doi.org/10.1080/01596306.2014.888838.

Gross, Terry, and Joshua Green. 2016. "Journalist Says Steve Bannon Had A 'Years-Long Plan' To Take Down Hillary Clinton." *NPR*, November 17. https://www.npr.org/2016/11/17/502413784/journalist-says-steve-bannon-had-a-years-long-plan-to-take-down-hillary-clinton.

Grossberg, Lawrence. 1986. "Is There Rock After Punk?" *Critical Studies in Mass Communication* 3 (1): 50–74. https://doi.org/10.1080/15295038609366629.

Halberstam, Jack. 2011. *The Queer Art of Failure*. Durham: Duke University Press.

Hale, Grace Elizabeth. 1999. *Making Whiteness: The Culture of Segregation in the South, 1890 - 1940*. New York: Vintage Books.

Hall, Stuart. 2021. *Selected Writings on Race and Difference*. Edited by Paul Gilroy and Ruth Wilson Gilmore. Durham: Duke University Press.

Halpern, Orit. 2014. *Beautiful Data: A History of Vision and Reason since 1945*. Durham: Duke University Press.

Haney-López, Ian. 1996. *White by Law: The Legal Construction of Race*. New York: New York University Press.

Haraway, Donna. 1990. "A Manifesto for Cyborgs: Science, Technology, and Socialist Feminism in the 1980s." In *Feminism/Postmodernism*, edited by Linda Nicholson, 190–223. New York: Routledge.

Harris, Cheryl I. 1993. "Whiteness as Property." *Harvard Law Review* 106 (8): 1707.

Hartman, Saidiya V. 2019. *Wayward Lives, Beautiful Experiments: Intimate Histories of Social Upheaval*. New York: W.W. Norton & Company.

Hausman, Bernice L. 2019. *Anti/Vax: Reframing the Vaccine Controversy*. Ithaca, NY: Cornell University Press.

Heaven, Will Douglas. 2020. "A GPT-3 Bot Posted Comments on Reddit for a Week and No One Noticed." *MIT Technology Review*. October 8. https://www.technologyreview.com/2020/10/08/1009845/a-gpt-3-bot-posted-comments-on-reddit-for-a-week-and-no-one-noticed/.

Hebdige, Dick. 2012. *Subculture: The Meaning of Style*. Hoboken: Taylor and Francis.

Hegel, Georg Wilhelm Friedrich. [1807] 1979. *Phenomenology of Spirit*. Edited by A. V. Miller and John N. Findlay. Oxford: Oxford University Press.

Heidegger, Martin. 2013. *Being and Time*. Edited by Edward Robinson. Translated by John Macquarrie. Malden: Blackwell.

Heritage, Canadian. 2021. "Events in Asian Canadian History." https://www.canada.ca/en/canadian-heritage/campaigns/asian-heritage-month/important-events.html.

Herman, Edward S., and Noam Chomsky. 2002. "A Propaganda Model." In *Manufacturing Consent: The Political Economy of the Mass Media*, 1–35. New York: Pantheon Books.

Hester, Helen. 2018. *Xenofeminism*. Hoboken: John Wiley & Sons.

Higgins, Michael. 2019. "The Donald: Media, Celebrity, Authenticity, and Accountability." In *Trump's Media War*, edited by Catherine Happer, Andrew Hoskins, and William Merrin, 129–41. Cham: Springer International Publishing. https://doi.org/10.1007/978-3-319-94069-4_9.

Holt, Jennifer. 2011. *Empires of Entertainment: Media Industries and the Politics of Deregulation, 1980-1996*. New Brunswick: Rutgers University Press.

Hong, Sun-ha. 2016. "Data's Intimacy: Machinic Sensibility and the Quantified Self." *Communication +1* 5 (1): 1–36.

Honneth, Axel. 2018. *The Struggle for Recognition: The Moral Grammar of Social Conflicts*. Oxford: Polity Press.

———, Judith Butler, Raymond Geuss, Jonathan Lear, and Martin Jay. 2008. *Reification: A New Look at an Old Idea*. Oxford; New York: Oxford University Press.

Horton, Donald, and R. Richard Wohl. 1956. "Mass Communication and Para-Social Interaction: Observations on Intimacy at a Distance." *Psychiatry* 19 (3): 215–29. https://doi.org/10.1080/00332747.1956.11023049.

Howe, LeAnne. 1999. "Tribalography: The Power of Native Stories." *Journal of Dramatic Theory and Criticism*, 117–26.

"Identification, n." n.d. *OED Online*. Oxford University Press.

Jagose, Annamarie. 1996. *Queer Theory: An Introduction*. New York: New York University Press.

Jameson, Fredric. 2005. *Postmodernism, or, The Cultural Logic of Late Capitalism*. Durham: Duke University Press.

Johnson, E. Patrick. 2003. *Appropriating Blackness: Performance and the Politics of Authenticity*. Durham: Duke University Press.

———, and Ramón H. Rivera-Servera, eds. 2016. *Blacktino Queer Performance*. Durham: Duke University Press.

Joque, Justin. 2018. *Deconstruction Machines: Writing in the Age of Cyberwar*. Minneapolis: University of Minnesota Press.

Karlova, Natascha A., and Karen E. Fisher. 2013. "A Social Diffusion Model of Misinformation and Disinformation for Understanding Human Information Behaviour." *Inf Res* 18.

Keeling, Kara. 2007. *The Witch's Flight: The Cinematic, the Black Femme, and the Image of Common Sense*. Durham: Duke University Press.

Kelley, Robin D. G. 1999. "Playing for Keeps: Pleasure and Profit on the Postindustrial Playground." In *The House That Race Built: Original Essays by Toni Morrison, Angela Y. Davis, Cornel West, and Others on Black Americans and Politics in America Today*, edited by Wahneema H. Lubiano. New York: Vintage Books.

Koffler, Keith. 2015. "The Authentic Trump." *LifeZette*. https://www.lifezette.com/2015/08/the-authentic-trump/.

Kor-Sins, Ryan. 2021. "The Alt-Right Digital Migration: A Heterogeneous Engineering Approach to Social Media Platform Branding." *New Media & Society*, August. https://doi.org/10.1177/14614448211038810.

Kotz, Liz. 1992. "The Body You Want: An Interview with Judith Butler." *Artforum* 31 (3).

Kunz, William M. 2007. *Culture Conglomerates: Consolidation in the Motion Picture and Television Industries*. Rowman & Littlefield.

Lacan, Jacques. 2006. "The Mirror Stage as Formative of the I Function as Revealed in Psychoanalytic Experience." In *Ecrits: The First Complete Edition in English*, translated by Bruce Fink, 75–81. New York: W.W. Norton & Co.

Laclau, Ernesto. 2014. *The Rhetorical Foundations of Society*. London; New York: Verso.

Latour, Bruno. 2004. "Why Has Critique Run Out of Steam? From Matters of Fact to Matters of Concern." *Critical Inquiry* 30 (2): 225–48. https://doi.org/10.1086/421123.

Le, Quynh Nhu. 2019. *Unsettled Solidarities: Asian and Indigenous Cross-Representations in the Américas*. Philadelphia: Temple University Press.

Le Zotte, Jennifer. 2017. "Connoisseurs of Trash in a World Full of It." In *From Goodwill to Grunge: A History of Secondhand Styles and Alternative Economies*, 214–38. Durham: University of North Carolina Press.

Leon, Adrian De. 2020. "The Long History of US Racism Against Asian Americans, from 'Yellow Peril' to 'Model Minority' to the 'Chinese Virus'." *The Conversation*. http://theconversation.com/the-long-history-of-us-racism-against-asian-americans-from-yellow-peril-to-model-minority-to-the-chinese-virus-135793.

Lewis, Rebecca. 2020. '"This Is What the News Won't Show You": YouTube Creators and the Reactionary Politics of Micro-Celebrity'. *Television & New Media* 21 (2): 201–17. https://doi.org/10.1177/1527476419879919.

Lorey, Isabell, and Judith Butler. 2015. *State of Insecurity: Government of the Precarious*. Translated by Aileen Derieg. London; New York: Verso Books.

Loukissas, Yanni A. 2019. *All Data Are Local: Thinking Critically in a Data-Driven Society*. Cambridge, MA: The MIT Press.

Lubiano, Wahneema. 1996. "Like Being Mugged by a Metaphor: Multiculturalism and State Narratives." In *Mapping Multiculturalism*, 64–75. Minneapolis: University of Minnesota Press.

———. 1998. *The House That Race Built: Original Essays by Toni Morrison, Angela Y. Davis, Cornel West, and Others on Black Americans and Politics in America Today*. New York: Vintage Books.

Luoma-aho, Vilma, Tuisku Pirttimäki, Devdeep Maity, Juha Munnukka, and Hanna Reinikainen. 2019. 'Primed Authenticity: How Priming Impacts Authenticity Perception of Social Media Influencers'. *International Journal of Strategic Communication* 13 (4): 352–65. https://doi.org/10.1080/1553118X.2019.1617716.

Mackenzie, Adrian. 2006. *Cutting Code: Software and Sociality*. New York: Peter Lang.

MacKinnon, Catharine A. 1987. *Feminism Unmodified: Discourses on Life and Law*. Cambridge: Harvard University Press.

Manovich, Lev. 1999. "Database as Symbolic Form." *Convergence* 5 (2): 80–99. https://doi.org/10.1177/135485659900500206.

Markoff, John. 2005. *What the Dormouse Said: How the Sixties Counterculture Shaped the Personal Computer Industry*. New York: Viking.

Marres, Noortje. 2018. "Why We Can't Have Our Facts Back." *Engaging Science, Technology, and Society* 4 (July): 423–43. https://doi.org/10.17351/ests2018.188.

Martin, Susan E. 1994. "'Outsider Within' the Station House: The Impact of Race and Gender on Black Women Police." *Social Problems* 41 (3): 383–400. https://doi.org/10.2307/3096969.

Marwick, Alice Emily. 2013. *Status Update: Celebrity, Publicity, and Branding in the Social Media Age*. New Haven: Yale University Press.

Marx, Karl. 1981. *Capital: a critique of political economy*. Edited by Ben Fowkes and David Fernbach. London; New York: Penguin Books in association with New Left Review.

Matrix, VNS. 1991. "The Cyberfeminist Manifesto for the 21st Century." *VNS Matrix*. https://vnsmatrix.net/projects/the-cyberfeminist-manifesto-for-the-21st-century.

McCarthy, E. Doyle. 2009. "Emotional Performances as Dramas of Authenticity." In *Authenticity in Culture, Self, and Society*, edited by Phillip Vannini and J. Patrick Williams, 241–55. Farnham, England; Burlington, VT: Ashgate Pub.

McIntyre, Lee C. 2018. *Post-Truth*. Cambridge, MA: The MIT Press.

McManus, Doyle. 2015. "Campaign 2016's Quixotic Quest for 'Authenticity'." *Chicago Tribune*, November 2. https://www.chicagotribune.com/opinion/commentary/ct-bernie-sanders-donald-trump-authenticity-20151102-story.html.

McQuillan, Dan. 2018. "Data Science as Machinic Neoplatonism." *Philosophy & Technology* 31 (2): 253–72. https://doi.org/10.1007/s13347-017-0273-3.

Meyers, Erin. 2009. "'Can You Handle My Truth?': Authenticity and the Celebrity Star Image." *The Journal of Popular Culture* 42 (5): 890–907. https://doi.org/10.1111/j.1540-5931.2009.00713.x.

Mill, John Stuart. 1998. *On Liberty and Other Essays*. Edited by John Gray. Oxford; New York: Oxford University Press.

Montgomery, Martin. 2017. "Post-Truth Politics? Authenticity, Populism and the Electoral Discourses of Donald Trump." *Journal of Language & Politics* 16 (4): 619–39. https://doi.org/10.1075/jlp.17023.mon.

Moore, Ryan. 2004. "Postmodernism and Punk Subculture: Cultures of Authenticity and Deconstruction." *The Communication Review* 7 (3): 305–27. https://doi.org/10.1080/10714420490492238.

Morrison, Toni. 1993. *Playing in the Dark: Whiteness and the Literary Imagination*. New York: Vintage Books.

Mukerji, Chandra. 2007. "A Message from the Chair." *Newsletter of the Sociology of Culture Section of the American Sociological Association* 21 (3): 1.

Munn, Luke. 2019. "Algorithmic Hate: Brenton Tarrant and the Dark Social Web." *Institute of Network Cultures*, March. https://networkcultures.org/blog/2019/03/19/luke-munn-algorithmic-hate-brenton-tarrant-and-the-dark-social-web/.

Namaste, Ki. 1996. "Genderbashing: Sexuality, Gender, and the Regulation of Public Space." *Environment and Planning D: Society and Space* 14 (2): 221–40. https://doi.org/10.1068/d140221.

Nash, Jennifer C. 2020. "Black Feminine Enigmas, or Notes on the Politics of Black Feminist Theory." *Signs: Journal of Women in Culture and Society* 45 (3): 519–23. https://doi.org/10.1086/706432.

Nygren, Gunnar, and Andreas Widholm. 2018. "Changing Norms Concerning Verification." In *Trust in Media and Journalism*, edited by Kim Otto and Andreas Köhler, 39–59. Wiesbaden: Springer Fachmedien Wiesbaden. https://doi.org/10.1007/978-3-658-20765-6_3.

Nyong'o, Tavia. 2014. "Unburdening Representation." *The Black Scholar* 44 (2): 70–80. https://doi.org/10.1080/00064246.2014.11413689.

Ode, Karl. 2021. "Hacked Facebook Users Forced To Buy $300 Oculus VR Headset Just To Talk To Customer Support." *Techdirt*. August. https://www.techdirt.com/2021/08/11/hacked-facebook-users-forced-to-buy-300-oculus-vr-headset-just-to-talk-to-customer-support/.

Oehmichen, Axel, Kevin Hua, Julio Amador Díaz López, Miguel Molina-Solana, Juan Gómez-Romero, and Yi-ke Guo. 2019. "Not All Lies Are Equal. A Study Into the Engineering of Political Misinformation in the 2016 US Presidential Election." *IEEE Access* 7: 126305–14. https://doi.org/10.1109/ACCESS.2019.2938389.

Orvell, Miles. 1989. *The Real Thing: Imitation and Authenticity in American Culture, 1880-1940*. Chapel Hill: University of North Carolina Press.

Osman, Suleiman. 2011. *The Invention of Brownstone Brooklyn: Gentrification and the Search for Authenticity in Postwar New York*. Oxford; New York: Oxford University Press.

Oxford Languages. 2016. "Post-Truth." *Oxford Word of the Year*. https://languages.oup.com/word-of-the-year/2016/.

Palumbo-Liu, David. 1999. *Asian/American: Historical Crossings of a Racial Frontier*. Stanford: Stanford University Press.

Parisi, Luciana. 2016. "Do Algorithms Have Fun? On Completion. Indeterminacy, and Autonomy in Computation." In *Fun and Software: Exploring Pleasure, Paradox, and Pain in Computing*, edited by Olga Goriunova. New York; London; Oxford: Bloomsbury Academic.

———. 2019. "The Alien Subject of AI"' *Subjectivity* 12 (1): 27–48. https://doi.org/10.1057/s41286-018-00064-3.

Phelan, Peggy. 1993. *Unmarked: The Politics of Performance*. London; New York: Routledge.

Poovey, Mary. 1998. *A History of the Modern Fact: Problems of Knowledge in the Sciences of Wealth and Society*. Chicago: University of Chicago Press.

Pornin, Thomas. 2011. "Cryptography - How Does RSA Encryption Compare to PGP?" *Information Security Stack Exchange*. https://web.archive.org/web/20160311152328/https://security.stackexchange.com/questions/1750/how-does-rsa-encryption-compare-to-pgp.

Povinelli, Elizabeth A. 2002. *The Cunning of Recognition: Indigenous Alterities and the Making of Australian Multiculturalism*. Durham: Duke University Press. https://doi.org/10.1215/9780822383673.

Preciado, Paul B. 2014. *Pornotopia: An Essay on Playboy's Architecture and Biopolitics*. New York: Zone Books.

———. 2018. *Countersexual Manifesto*. New York: Columbia University Press.

Puar, Jasbir. 2013. "Rethinking Homonationalism." *International Journal of Middle East Studies* 45 (2): 336–39. https://doi.org/10.1017/S002074381300007X.

Rabin, Nathan. 2006. "Stephen Colbert." *The A.V. Club*, January. https://www.avclub.com/stephen-colbert-1798208958.

Raibmon, P. 2005. *Authentic Indians: Episodes of Encounter from the Late-Nineteenth-Century Northwest Coast*. Duke University Press.

Reynolds, Simon. 2010. *Totally Wired: Post-Punk Interviews and Overviews*. 1st American edition. New York: Soft Skull Press.

Rivest, R. L., A. Shamir, and L. Adleman. 1978. "A Method for Obtaining Digital Signatures and Public-Key Cryptosystems." *Communications of the ACM* 21 (2): 120–26. https://doi.org/10.1145/359340.359342.

Roediger, David R. 2007. *The Wages of Whiteness: Race and the Making of the American Working Class*. Edited by Mike Davis and Michael Sprinker. London; New York: Verso.

Romeo, Nick, and Ian Tewksbury. 2019. "Trump Personifies Emerson's Idea of the 'Authentic' Man." *The Daily Beast*, November 28. https://www.thedailybeast.com/another-good-reason-to-loathe-ralph-waldo-emerson-trump/.

Rose, Tricia. 1994. *Black Noise: Rap Music and Black Culture in Contemporary America*. Middletown, CT: Wesleyan University Press.

———. 1996. "A Style Nobody Can Deal With: Politics, Style and the Postindustrial City in Hip Hop." In *Mapping Multiculturalism*, 424–44. Minneapolis: University of Minnesota Press.

Rosenwald, Brian. 2019. *Talk Radio's America: How an Industry Took Over a Political Party That Took Over the United States*. Cambridge, MA: Harvard University Press. https://doi.org/10.4159/9780674243224.

Rossinow, Douglas C. 1998. *The Politics of Authenticity: Liberalism, Christianity, and the New Left in America*. New York: Columbia University Press.

Rousseau, Jean-Jacques. 1903. *The Confessions of Jean Jacques Rousseau*. London: Aldus Society.

Rubin, Gayle. 2011. *Deviations: A Gayle Rubin Reader*. Durham: Duke University Press.

Schechner, Richard. 2017. *Performance Studies: An Introduction*. 3rd ed. Abingdon: Routledge. https://doi.org/10.4324/9780203125168.

Senft, Theresa M. 2008. *Camgirls: Celebrity and Community in the Age of Social Networks*. New York: Peter Lang.

Shakespeare, William. [1623] 2010. *As You Like It*. Edited by Jonathan Bate and Eric Rasmussen. 2010 Modern Library pbk. ed. New York: Modern Library.

Shapin, Steven. 1994. *A Social History of Truth: Civility and Science in Seventeenth-Century England*. Chicago: University of Chicago Press.

Shimakawa, Karen. 2002. *National Abjection: The Asian American Body Onstage*. Durham: Duke University Press.

Shreyas, Reddy. 2020. "K-Pop Fans Emerge as a Powerful Force in US Protests." *BBC News*, June. https://www.bbc.com/news/world-asia-52996705.

Sorensen, Eric. 1998. "Asian Groups Attack MSNBC Headline Referring To Kwan – News Web Site Apologizes For Controversial Wording." *The Seattle Times*, March 3.

Starbird, Kate, Ahmer Arif, Tom Wilson, Katherine Van Koevering, Katya Yefimova, and Daniel Scarnecchia. 2018. "Ecosystem or Echo-System? Exploring Content Sharing Across Alternative Media Domains." In *Proceedings of the International AAAI Conference on Web and Social Media* 12 (1). https://doi.org/10.1609/icwsm.v12i1.15009

Strong, Catherine. 2016. *Grunge: Music and Memory*. Abington: Routledge. https://doi.org/10.4324/9781315585994.

Stryker, Susan. 2004. "Transgender Studies: Queer Theory's Evil Twin." *GLQ: A Journal of Lesbian and Gay Studies* 10 (2): 212–15.

Sundén, Jenny. 2015. "On Trans-, Glitch, and Gender as Machinery of Failure." *First Monday*, March. https://doi.org/10.5210/fm.v20i4.5895.

Swire, Briony, Adam J. Berinsky, Stephan Lewandowsky, and Ullrich K. H. Ecker. 2017. "Processing Political Misinformation: Comprehending the Trump Phenomenon." *Royal Society Open Science* 4 (3): 160802. https://doi.org/10.1098/rsos.160802.

Szalai, Jennifer. 2016. "What Makes a Politician 'Authentic'?" *The New York Times*, July 5.

Talbot, William Henry Fox. 1843. "Some Account of the Art of Photogenic Drawing, or the Process by Which Natural Objects May Be Made to Delineate Themselves

Without the Aid of the Artist's Pencil." *Abstracts of the Papers Printed in the Philosophical Transactions of the Royal Society of London* 4 (December): 120–21. https://doi.org/10.1098/rspl.1837.0051.

TallBear, Kim. 2013. *Native American DNA: Tribal Belonging and the False Promise of Genetic Science*. Minneapolis: University of Minnesota Press.

Totaro, Paolo, and Domenico Ninno. 2014. "The Concept of Algorithm as an Interpretative Key of Modern Rationality." *Theory, Culture & Society* 31 (4): 29–49. https://doi.org/10.1177/0263276413510051.

Taylor, Charles. 1992. *The Ethics of Authenticity*. Cambridge, MA: Harvard University Press.

Thornton, Sarah. 1996. *Club Cultures: Music, Media, and Subcultural Capital*. 1st U.S. ed. Hanover: University Press of New England.

Trilling, Lionel. 1972. *Sincerity and Authenticity*. Cambridge, MA: Harvard University Press.

Turner, Fred. 2006. *From Counterculture to Cyberculture: Stewart Brand, the Whole Earth Network, and the Rise of Digital Utopianism*. Chicago: University of Chicago Press.

———. 2019. "Trump on Twitter: How a Medium Designed for Democracy Became an Authoritarian's Mouthpiece." In *Antidemocracy in America*, 83–92. New York: Columbia University Press. https://doi.org/10.7312/klin19010-011.

Ward, Elizabeth Jane. 2015. *Not Gay: Sex Between Straight White Men*. New York: New York University Press.

Watson, Philip. 2020. "r/NoStupidQuestions - Comment by u/Pbw on 'How Does This User Post so Many Large, Deep Posts so Rapidly?'". Reddit. October 4. https://www.reddit.com/r/NoStupidQuestions/comments/j4xhz6/how_does_this_user_post_so_many_large_deep_posts/g704lem.

Wilde, Oscar. 2000. *The Complete Works of Oscar Wilde*. Edited by Josephine M. Guy. Oxford; New York: Oxford University Press.

Williams, Raymond. 2011. *The Long Revolution*. Cardigan: Parthian Books.

Willis, Paul E. 2014. *Profane Culture*. Princeton: Princeton University Press.

Winnicott, D. W. 1953. "Transitional Objects and Transitional Phenomena; a Study of the First Not-Me Possession." *The International Journal of Psycho-Analysis* 34 (2): 89–97.

Wirth, R. 2014. "The Revolutionary Encounter." In *Mestizaje and Globalization: Transformations of Identity and Power*, edited by Stefanie Wickstrom and Philip D. Young, 25–42. Tucson, AZ: University of Arizona Press.

Wolfe, Tom. 1976. "The 'Me' Decade and the Third Great Awakening." *New York Magazine*, August 23.

Wynne, Brian. 1992. "Misunderstood Misunderstanding: Social Identities and Public Uptake of Science." *Public Understanding of Science* 1 (3): 281–304. https://doi.org/10.1088/0963-6625/1/3/004.

Young, Cynthia A. 2019. "Becked Up: Glenn Beck, White Supremacy, and the Hijacking of the Civil Rights Legacy." In *Racism Postrace*, 86–112. Durham: Duke University Press. https://doi.org/10.1515/9781478003250-006.

Young, Ian. 2014. "Putting Canada First Drops Anti-Asian Activist Bradley Saltzberg over Fake IDs." *South China Morning Post.* September 29. https://www.scmp.com/news/world/article/1603444/putting-canada-first-drops-anti-asian-activist-bradley-saltzberg-over.

Zeman, Z. A. B. 1973. *Nazi Propaganda.* 2nd ed. London; New York: Oxford University Press.

Authors

Liliana Bounegru is Lecturer in Digital Methods at the Department of Digital Humanities, King's College London, co-founder of the Public Data Lab and affiliated with the Digital Methods Initiative in Amsterdam and the médialab, Sciences Po in Paris. More about her work can be found at lilianabounegru.org.

Anthony Glyn Burton is a Mellon-SFU Data Fluencies Fellow at the Digital Democracies Institute and a PhD Candidate in the School of Communication at Simon Fraser University.

Wendy Hui Kyong Chun is Simon Fraser University's Canada 150 Research Chair in New Media and Professor of Communication and Director of the SFU Digital Democracies Institute. Her last book is Discriminating Data: Correlation, Neighborhoods, and the New Politics of Recognition (MIT Press).

Melody Devries is a PhD candidate in the Communication & Culture Department at Toronto Metropolitan University. She uses ethnographic methods to analyze processes of political conviction online.

Amy Harris is a PhD candidate in the School of Communication at Simon Fraser University and a researcher at the Digital Democracies Institute. Her research focuses on how museums and exhibitions about climate change help people to understand what the future will look like.

hannah holtzclaw is a Ph.D. student in the School of Communications, as well as a Data Fluencies Fellow to the Digital Democracies Institute, at Simon Fraser University.

Ioana B. Jucan is a scholar and artis. Juncan is Assistant Professor of Social and Cultural Inquiry at Emerson College and the author of Malicious Deceivers: Thinking Machines and Performative Objects (Stanford University Press, 2023).

Alexandra Juhasz is distinguished professor of film at Brooklyn College, CUNY.

D. W. Kamish is a PhD student in the School of Communication at Simon Fraser University and researcher at the Digital Democracies Institute.

Ganaele Langlois is Associate Professor in the Department of Communication and Media Studies at York University, Canada. Her research areas are: digital cultures, digital methods, and critical media theory.

Jasmine Proctor (she/they) is an independent researcher whose work focuses on the intersection of identity, labour, and fandom. Her previous work has focused on how the relationship between fan labour, government policy, and corporate strategy has allowed for Korean popular music to be leveraged as a soft power tool.

Christine Tomlinson is a lecturer and researcher in the School of Social Sciences at the University of California, Irvine investigating online cultures and interaction, video game players' experiences, and video game content. Christine previously worked as a game studies specialist with the Digital Democracies Institute at Simon Fraser University.

Roopa Vasudevan is a new media artist, computer programmer and researcher whose work examines social and technological defaults; interrogates rules, conventions and protocols that we often ignore or take for granted; and centers humanity and community in explorations of technology's impacts on society. Her current academic research investigates the complex and involved relationships between new media artists and the tech industry.

Esther Weltevrede is Assistant Professor of New Media and Digital Culture at the University of Amsterdam, and a member of the Digital Methods Initiative and the App Studies Initiative. Her research is supported by the Dutch Research Council (NWO), project number VI.Veni.191C.048.

www.ingramcontent.com/pod-product-compliance
Ingram Content Group UK Ltd.
Pitfield, Milton Keynes, MK11 3LW, UK
UKHW041952190726
13854UKWH00005B/1914